DEVIL'S ADVOCATES

DEVIL'S ADVOCATES is a series of books devoted to exploring the classics of horror cinema. Contributors to the series come from the fields of teaching, academia, journalism and fiction, but all have one thing in common: a passion for the horror film and a desire to share it with the widest possible audience.

'The admirable Devil's Advocates series is not only essential – and fun – reading for the serious horror fan but should be set texts on any genre course.'
Dr Ian Hunter, Reader in Film Studies, De Montfort University, Leicester

'Auteur Publishing's new Devil's Advocates critiques on individual titles... offer bracingly fresh perspectives from passionate writers. The series will perfectly complement the BFI archive volumes.' **Christopher Fowler, *Independent on Sunday***

'Devil's Advocates has proven itself more than capable of producing impassioned, intelligent analyses of genre cinema... quickly becoming the go-to guys for intelligent, easily digestible film criticism.' ***Horror Talk.com***

'Auteur Publishing continue the good work of giving serious critical attention to significant horror films.' ***Black Static***

 DevilsAdvocatesbooks

DevilsAdBooks

Also available in this series

Antichrist Amy Simmonds

Black Sunday Martyn Conterio

Carrie Neil Mitchell

The Curse of Frankenstein Marcus K. Harmes

Dead of Night Jez Conolly & David Bates

The Descent James Marriot

Halloween Murray Leeder

Let the Right One In Anne Billson

Saw Benjamin Poole

The Silence of the Lambs Barry Forshaw

Suspiria Alexandra Heller-Nicholas

The Texas Chain Saw Massacre James Rose

The Thing Jez Conolly

Witchfinder General Ian Cooper

Forthcoming

Cannibal Holocaust Calum Waddell

Frenzy Ian Cooper

Near Dark John Berra

Psychomania I.Q. Hunter & Jamie Sherry

DEVIL'S ADVOCATES

NOSFERATU
A SYMPHONY OF HORROR

CRISTINA MASSACCESI

Acknowledgments

This book owes much to the excellent studies and analyses on F.W. Murnau and his films that have been published before my contribution. To them and their authors goes all my gratitude and admiration.

On a more personal note, I would like to thank Auteur's John Atkinson for his support and patience during the writing up of this book. I would also like to extend my heartfelt thanks to my partner, Anthony Davie, for the precious advice he gave me whenever I had to face the discussion of music-related issues, and to my brother, Francesco Massaccesi, for the stream of great research, material and ideas that he sent my way during preparation and writing up. A big thank you goes across the ocean to Howard S. Berger who put me in touch with E. Elias Merhige and, of course, to Elias himself who's been amazingly inspiring and willing to discuss his film at length with me. And last but not least, thanks to all my wonderful friends who have spurred me on throughout this project.

This book is dedicated to my mother, Elisa (1951–2010) and my father, Augusto.

auteur

First published in 2015 by
Auteur, 24 Hartwell Crescent, Leighton Buzzard LU7 1NP
www.auteur.co.uk
Copyright © Auteur 2015

Series design: Nikki Hamlett at Cassels Design
Set by Cassels Design www.casselsdesign.co.uk
Printed and bound by CPI Group (UK) Ltd, Croydon, CR0 4YY

British Library Cataloguing-in-Publication Data
A catalogue record for this book is available from the British Library

ISBN paperback: 978-0-9932384-5-1
ISBN ebook: 978-0-9932384-6-8

CONTENTS

Preface by E. Elias Merhige 7

Introduction 9

Film Synopsis 11

Chapter 1: Contexts 13
1.1 The political and social contexts of the Weimar Republic 13
1.2 The Weimar cinematographic industry 16
1.3 The German Expressionist movement 17
1.4 The stylistic traits of Expressionist cinema 18

Chapter 2: Bringing the Undead to Life 21
2.1 The film's crew 21
2.2 Production and reception 26
2.3 Controversy and legal action 29
2.4 From the page to the screen 32

Chapter 3: Reading the Vampire 41
3.1 The film on DVD 41
3.2 Reading *Nosferatu* as a 'complex discovery plot' 44

Chapter 4: Signs and Meanings 83
4.1 *Nosferatu*'s style and form 83
4.2 Interpretations 92

Chapter 5: *Nosferatu*'s Afterlives 103
5.1 Between tribute and alienation: Herzog's *Nosferatu. Phantom der Nacht* 104
5.2 The artist as despot: Merhige's *Shadow of the Vampire* 107

Appendix: Interview with E. Elias Merhige 113

Notes 121

Bibliography 125

Nosferatu film poster, designed by producer and set designer Albin Grau

PREFACE

The appearance of *Nosferatu* in 1922 is the first appearance ever of a vampire in the cinema. The impact of this film has never really been given its proper place in the history of cinema. It represents an articulation of the supernatural that was previously relegated to literature.

Nosferatu is what I would call an *experimental* film (I mean this as the highest compliment), because nothing like it before existed. Its use of technology and makeup, composition and lighting is so extraordinary that the filmmaking itself is 'supernatural' given the technology of film stock and lighting and cameras/lenses of that period. The novel use of real locations, taking the camera outside of the comfort zone of a studio setting, was something that many filmmakers saw as ridiculous and far too cumbersome at that time. The fact that Murnau chooses to explore the supernatural and the uncanny using real locations set in Nature as opposed to the artificial world one could create in a studio setting represents a remarkable and visionary turn in how films are made.

It is curious to know that at the time *Nosferatu* was made, the Stoker family felt it a demeaning embarrassment to adapt *Dracula* to the cinema screen, thus showing how early cinema was looked upon as a 'questionable' art not worthy of well-healed cultured audiences. This only magnifies just how forward thinking Murnau was in making *Nosferatu*.

I remember when I was twelve watching *Nosferatu* and being completely haunted by this film especially by its main character played by Max Schreck. The night scene at the castle, when the vampire shows up at Hutter's bedroom, strikes the most atavistic terror into the heart of the audience and it is a scene that has never left me. The vampire's insect-like movements, the stiff and laboured motion of the limbs, the unnaturally extended long fingers, the unblinking piercing rat-like eyes and teeth compounded by the enlarged bald head made this creature horrifying and unforgettable.

In my own research on Murnau for *Shadow of the Vampire*, it had upset me a great deal to learn that almost half of his films are completely 'lost' and totally unaccounted for. Where have they gone? And why are they missing? It is very interesting to know that the Stoker estate sued Prana films, the production company Albin Grau, the film's producer, and Murnau formed together to make *Nosferatu* at the time. The Stoker estate won and *Nosferatu* was declared illegal and wrong to have been made. A court order was issued in which all the original negatives were to be burned along with existing prints of the film. *Nosferatu* was to be erased from the earth. So how does the film exist today? It exists only because a print that was unaccounted for in France was not found and burned at that time. Every print thereafter was from a negative struck from that print.

There are not many books on Murnau and even fewer books on *Nosferatu* specifically. It is my pleasure to introduce this book written by a passionate and brilliant young scholar, Cristina Massaccesi. I am delighted that her study is specifically devoted on this singular work of cinematic art – may it further inspire more to understand its ground-breaking levels of cinematic innovation, style and beauty and to discover even greater depth in Murnau's *Nosferatu*.

E. Elias Merhige
Los Angeles, 21 March 2015

INTRODUCTION

Nosferatu. Eine Symphonie des Grauens (*Nosferatu. A Symphony of Horror*) directed by German director Friedrich Wilhelm Murnau in 1922 is not only regarded as one of the most intriguing and disquieting films to have been produced during the years of Weimar cinema but can also be considered as a key step in establishing the vampire as a cinematic figure and in shaping its connection with our subconscious fears and desires. Appearing before and still to this day clearly contrasting later well-known cinematic figures – such as the black-clad Count Dracula interpreted by Bela Lugosi in Tod Browning's adaptation of 1931, Gary Oldman's love-torn hero of Francis Ford Coppola's 1992 rendition of Bram Stoker's novel, the Swedish child-vampire of *Let the Right One In* (2008) and the romantic Edward Cullen of the *Twilight* trilogy – Count Orlok can be considered the Ur-Vampire, the father of all undead creatures lurking in the darkest recesses of a cinema screen.

An enigmatic work, with a complex and elusive history, *Nosferatu* is highly ambiguous, full of allusions and echoes that still resonate more than ninety years after its completion and release. As pointed out by Thomas Elsaesser,

> *Nosferatu* […] convey[s] the sense of a narrative at once simple, because of folk-legend, fairy-tale 'inevitability', and mysterious, because the overall meaning and shape remain inaccessible to linear cause-effect logic.[1]

A compelling example of poetic cinema progressing through secret affinities and correspondences rather than a prosaic story of horrific events and adventure, its chilling advancement towards a tragic climax is built along the lines of what can now be seen as a classic vampire story made familiar to audiences through an infinite number of books, adaptations and films. However, when it was released in 1922, *Nosferatu* was an absolute novelty not simply as a horror film but also in terms of Expressionist – and more generally cinematographic – aesthetics and narrative. As we shall see in the relevant section of this book, its very connection with Expressionist cinema has been widely contested and discussed not simply because Weimar cinema is too diversified and contradictory to fit neatly under one umbrella term but also because *Nosferatu* presents a series of features and motives that seem to arch back all the way to German Romanticism. Furthermore, its inextricable connection with the visual arts – that range from Caspar David Friedrich to Alfred Böcklin, from Giorgio De Chirico to Carl Spitzweg and numerous others – makes it a multifaceted and complex canvas and I believe it is this underlying complexity the ultimate reason of its enduring allure. As effectively pointed out by Tom Gunning in an article published in 2007,

> *Nosferatu* explored the play between the visible and the invisible, reflections and shadow, on- and off-screen space that cinema made possible, forging a technological image of the uncanny. One senses throughout *Nosferatu* this excitement of innovation, of redefining a medium by testing and transforming its relation to its own history and to other media (the strong use Murnau makes of painting, literary texts, scientific discourse, and even musical rhythms).[2]

Furthermore, as the first or at least the earliest surviving attempt at adapting Bram Stoker's *Dracula* (1897) for the screen, if we exclude an earlier Hungarian film that is now completely lost,[3] *Nosferatu* established a series of conventions that would shape cinema audiences' expectations and relationship to cinematic vampires for decades to come.

My personal fascination with *Nosferatu* goes back a long way and I can still remember vividly the sense of unease and fear that a late-night showing on Italian television instilled in me when I was a high-school student. Over the years the lurking shadow of Count Orlok has spread from my personal to my working life and I now regularly teach *Nosferatu* to my film adaptation students in the School of European languages, Culture and Society of University College London. The enthusiasm and reaction the film invariably triggers in the class never ceases to amaze me. Keeping this in mind, in the following text I will attempt to unravel the never-ending and quite literally undying fascination exercised by the film over generations of viewers and filmmakers whilst at the same time providing the reader with a clear and easy-to-follow guide about the film's contexts, cinematography, and possible interpretations. My hope is that this little contribution to the vast scholarship devoted to Murnau and his film will give to students and enthusiastic cinemagoers another reason to discover or further explore this work.

FILM SYNOPSIS

The young estate agent Hutter is sent by his shady employer Knock to a remote place in the Carpathian Mountains to close a deal with a local nobleman, Count Orlok, who wishes to buy a property in Wisborg. Knock suggests his employee to offer Count Orlok an empty building which is right opposite Hutter's home. After leaving his young wife Ellen, who appears to be particularly distressed at the thought of her husband's mission, in the care of their friend Harding and his sister (who is identified as Anny in the original script), Hutter leaves for his journey with great expectations and enthusiasm.

Once arrived in the Carpathians he spends a night with some local peasants who shudder and cross themselves at the mention of the very name of Orlok and forcefully invite him to give up on his journey. However, neither the peasants nor the warnings contained in a book on 'vampires, monstrous ghosts, sorcery, and the Seven Deadly Sins' found on his bedside table can dissuade Hutter from reaching Orlok's isolated castle. Left in the middle of the forest by the carriage men who refuse to accompany him any further, Hutter is picked up by a coach driven by a mysterious man completely wrapped up in a black cloak and eventually deposited at the entrance of the Count's castle. Once crossed the archway, the Count, who appears to be a lanky and pale figure clad in a tight black suit, meets Hutter and invites him into what appears to be a deserted home. During his first dinner with Orlok, Hutter cuts his finger with a breadknife and observes with shock the Count licking his lips seemingly in anticipation at the sight of his blood. During Hutter's second night at the castle Orlok attacks his guest in his room with the apparent intention of drinking his blood. At the same moment, Ellen wakes up and starts sleepwalking on the balustrade of Harding's villa. Although the doctor dismisses her state as a 'harmless congestion of the blood', an intertitle and a creative use of cross-editing link her illness to *Nosferatu*'s actions against Hutter and to the Count's forthcoming arrival in Wisborg. Back at the castle, Hutter is horrified in discovering that the count sleeps in a sarcophagus and then observes him loading up a cart with coffins and leaving the castle. Understanding Orlok's intention to go to Wisborg and thus linking the Count's arrival in town with an ominous sentiment of danger and alarm, Hutter escapes from the castle and is found feverish and confused by some local peasants. Meanwhile the crew of the schooner Empusa set sails to Wisborg oblivious of the danger lurking in the boat's load. A cut takes the viewer back to Wisborg where Professor Bulwer (whom we briefly saw at the beginning of the film when he admonished Hutter that 'no one can escape his destiny') is lecturing on carnivorous plants and other mysteries of nature whilst Hutter's employer Knock is showing clear signs of madness and Ellen is seen by the sea longing for her beloved. A new intertitle features a newspaper cut detailing the explosion of a plague epidemic in Transylvania and other ports on the Black Sea, whilst on the Empusa the sailors fall one by one victim of Count Orlok. The arrival in Wisborg of the now empty and spectral ship during one of the film's most spectacular and iconic sequences also marks the beginning of the plague for the town's inhabitants. Ellen, although breaching Hutter's explicit prohibition, reads an excerpt from the *Book of Vampires* and discovers that only the sacrifice of a woman without sin can put an end to the plague brought to the town by the *Nosferatu*. With the panic-stricken town crumbling around her, Ellen summons *Nosferatu* into her room and lets him drink her blood until the morning when the first ray of the sun kills the vampire thus freeing Wisborg from the curse. The last shot of the film shows us a distressed Hutter embracing his dead wife whilst in the image's foreground Professor Bulwer looks defeated and helpless.

CHAPTER 1 – CONTEXTS

1.1 THE POLITICAL AND SOCIAL CONTEXT OF THE WEIMAR REPUBLIC

Films can often become the expressive channel for the social, political, and cultural issues at work in a given time and place – we could think for example of Italian Neorealism and its role in providing a timely and faithful depiction of a country prostrated by twenty years of Fascist dictatorship and by the devastations of the war in the immediate aftermath of World War Two. From this point of view then, *Nosferatu*, along with many other of the films produced during the Weimar Republic and despite its apparent detachment from current events, can be doubtlessly interpreted as a vehicle to express the inner anxiety and unrest that were at work in Germany during the dramatic and unruly years that followed the end of the First World War. If we really want to fully understand the film then we also need to be able to orient ourselves around the political and historical events that were triggered by the defeat in the world conflict and that precipitated the social and political situation in the country. These occurrences also had a strong – and unexpectedly positive – impact over Germany's cultural and cinematographic output that once unrestricted from the stuffy and backward climate of the old imperial order, became free to innovate and experiment with unprecedented enthusiasm.

The world war of 1914-1918 slaughtered and wiped away a whole generation of young Europeans and it caused overall the death on the battlefields of about 10 million soldiers. Germany lost 2 million men during the fighting and 4.2 million returned home shell-shocked or horribly wounded and disfigured. Historians tell us that about 19 per cent of the entire German male population were direct casualties of the war's terrible violence. At the same time though, the war also triggered some direct or indirect drastic political changes in countries such as Russia – where the Tsarist regime was overthrown and replaced by a revolutionary government in 1917 – and Germany where Kaiser Wilhelm II and his government, pushed by a wave of revolts and strikes started by the sailors stationed in the port city of Kiel on 29 October 1918, were forced to step down on 9 November 1918 when the chancellorship was handed over to Friedrich Ebert, the secretary of the Social Democratic Party (SPD). Soon after the Kaiser's abdication the empire was replaced by the proclamation of the German Republic and the new government steered Germany's political direction towards a more democratic course by approving a series of decrees establishing freedom of speech, press and religion, universal suffrage and by also granting an amnesty for political prisoners still detained in the Kaiser's prisons. However, the first tentative steps of the new government were marred by political chaos and by the looming shadow of the peace treaty that was still being drafted by the victorious forces after Germany had signed the armistice in the French town of Compiègne on 11 November 1918. The winter months of 1918-1919 were a rollercoaster of events that saw Ebert working feverishly in the attempt of bringing together all the different forces that could have a say in the shaping up of Germany's political future. Furthermore, the ghost of another Bolshevik revolution stirred real panic in many sectors of German society, and the newly-appointed Chancellor knew that only appropriate political tools, namely elections and a new constitution, could legitimate the new government in the eyes of those citizens who feared a radical turn towards Communism. For this reason, Ebert struck a series of deals and compromises with the military, the capitalist elites and the old sectors of highly placed civil servants. In the long run, these deals and the overall negotiating approach taken by the Ebert cabinet proved to be fateful since 'once the sense of panic had passed, once officers, civilian officials, and capitalists felt the balance of power again shifting in their direction, they would look for other allies, which they found, ultimately, in the Nazi Party' that finally seized political power in January 1933.[4]

On 19 January 1919, German citizens were called to the polls to elect a Constitutional Convention. The Social Democrats, together with the Catholic Centre and other conservative parties with whom they shared their pleas for hard work, discipline and order, received the majority of the votes and Philip Scheidemann, the SPD representative who had seized the chance to declare the birth of the German Republic on the very day of the Kaiser's abdication, became the new Chancellor. After the elections, the Constitutional Convention retired to Weimar to draft the new constitution that, formally proclaimed on 11 August 1919, was sustained by liberal and democratic ideals that granted and protected basic liberties and social reforms. All this happened while radical Right and Left wing groups fought each other on the streets of all the major German cities.

The chaos that characterised German internal politics at the beginning of 1919 was to be made even worse by the release of the terms of the peace treaty that the victorious powers (Great Britain, United States, France, and Italy) were meanwhile drafting in Paris. Germany's representatives were summoned to Paris at the end of April and had to wait, in a climate of continuous humiliation and hostility, until the 7th of May before they could have the details of the treaty that the Allies wished to impose on the defeated nation. Initial hopes for a peace with 'no annexations, no contributions, no punitive damages' as ensured by American President Woodrow Wilson in a speech given in front of the American Congress in January 1918, were immediately crushed by the uncovering of the harsh reality of the treaty's details. Germany was to lose over a seventh of its pre-war territory, drastically decrease the size of its army, dispose entirely of its air force, renounce all its colonies and pay a yet-undetermined sum of money and goods – that Germany would never be able to repay in full – in reparations for being the sole responsible of the war tragedy according to article 231 in the treaty, the so-called 'war guilt clause'. Despite the outrage and the widespread protests back home, on 28 June 1919 two members of the German government officially ended the hostilities by signing the Versailles Treaty.

The Treaty of Versailles specified that a Reparation Commission would be set up in 1921 with the aim to evaluate Germany's resources and establish the final reparation figure – that eventually resulted in the request of 132 billion gold marks. In the meantime, though, Germany was still expected to pay over 20 billion marks made up of gold, commodities, goods, etc. as an initial compensation. The burdens imposed by the peace treaty gradually brought the unsteady German economy to a situation of financial chaos. Repaying the Allies with commodities caused the development of domestic shortages that subsequently triggered an unstoppable rise in the prices of all sorts of goods. The predictable result of this situation was a rampaging hyperinflation that finally saw the German mark sink from 50,000 to one dollar at the beginning of 1923 to around 6 billion to the dollar by the end of that same year. The preponderance of people inevitably suffered from this situation: soup kitchens, worsening living standards, and extensive unemployment accompanied the images of German citizens carrying wheelbarrows full of money to buy a pair of shoes or a loaf of bread. The suffering however, was not equally shared by all strata of German society: the big industrial conglomerates benefited from the inflation that encouraged export while at the same time discouraging import; German goods could be sold cheaply abroad and even internally, rather than saving, people tended to spend money as long as it was still worth something thus keeping production going.

1.2 THE WEIMAR CINEMATOGRAPHIC INDUSTRY

The German cinematic industry benefited from this state of affairs for a number of reasons. First of all, unlike other goods, films were readily available and people flocked to film theatres throughout the inflationary period. Furthermore, German production companies profited from the financial impossibility of importing films from abroad, an impossibility that was further strengthened by the ban on foreign film imports that had been established back in 1916 and that was to last until the very end of December 1920. Finally, foreign countries, especially those in South America and Eastern Europe, whilst not being able to afford costly Hollywood movies, could easily buy the much cheaper films arriving from Germany. The combination of these diverse factors boosted the productivity and also the sheer number of German producing companies that went from twenty-five in 1914 to about three hundred in 1921, a number that included one-off diminutive companies – very much like Albin Grau's Prana film – and giants such as the Universum Film Aktiengesellschaft, better known as UFA. The expansion and strengthening of the German cinematographic industry was not just a consequence of the financial circumstances of the post-war years but also benefited from the fact that, despite political and economic uncertainty, the Germany of the 1920s was a decidedly 'mass' society. The majority of its population lived in urban areas where they would conduct lives revolving around the workplace and the marketplace and in which the guarantee of receiving at least a minimal level of public education was virtually universal. The combination of these social changes with the technological innovations made from the end of the 1890s onwards made Weimar 'a cacophony of sounds, a dazzle of images'.[5] It may sound surreal that a society in the grips of rampant inflation and violent political rivalries could be at the same time so creative and produce so much in artistic and cinematographic terms. This apparent contradiction though adds another layer of interest to the films produced during those chaotic years – their metaphors and visual conundrums providing a fascinating if at times hard to decipher insight into those tumultuous events. In Ian Roberts' words: 'Weimar society created the ideal breeding-ground for an art form based fundamentally upon the *illusion* of reality'.[6]

But what kind of films did Germany produce and export during the Weimar years? Roughly speaking, we could divide German cinematic output into three large genres. The first of these was the so-called *spectacle* film which concentrated on the re-enactment of epic or historical events that involved impressive sets and frequent crowd scenes – all things that could be easily afforded during the inflationary period when studio back lots and extras could be hired at exceptionally low wages. At the opposite end of the spectrum we find the *Kammerspiel* film, chamber-dramas revolving around few characters and events and often filmed on a limited number of different sets. However, the most famous and largely influential German films of the period are those falling under the umbrella term of Expressionism, a diverse and multi-faceted label that despite internal shifts and differences, presents a series of recognisable characteristics such as the utilisation of stylised sets, the unrealistic style of the acting performances and the suggestive use of lights and shadows.

1.3 THE GERMAN EXPRESSIONIST MOVEMENT

Before becoming a cinematographic style, Expressionism was a well-established and recognisable tendency already present in German theatre and painting where it had started at the very beginning of the twentieth century as another modernist movement attempting to react against the predominance of realism in the arts. Two painting movements in particular are at the basis of what will later be recognised as Expressionism: *Der Blaue Reiter* (The Blue Rider) and *Die Brücke* (The Bridge). Franz Marc, Wassily Kandisky and Gabriele Münter founded *Der Blaue Reiter* in Munich in 1911 while *Die Brücke*, founded in 1906 and based in Dresden, grouped together a number of artists and intellectuals such as Ernst Ludwig Kirchner and Karl Schmidt-Rottluff.

As clearly visible in paintings such as *Girl with a Cat II* by Franz Marc (1912) and *Potsdamer Platz* (1914) by Ernst Ludwig Kirchner both movements were characterised by a preference for bright and unnatural colours that through the avoidance of nuances and realism outlined cartoonlike human and animal figures often surrounded by elongated and distorted natural or urban landscapes used to express a sense of isolation or to convey the dehumanisation brought about by urban life. Both artistic movements exercised a strong influence on Expressionist cinema in general and their impact is also clearly visible in *Nosferatu* where in the dramatic views of Wisborg stricken by the plague or in Ellen's solitary watches on the beach

> [...] we reencounter the horror about the modern condition that the members of *Die Brücke* expressed through their tortured canvases as well as the longing for something impossible or forever lost conveyed by the painters of *Der Blaue Reiter*.[7]

Expressionist theatre of the early twentieth century shared similar preoccupations with painters such as Marc and Kirchner. The plays by authors like Georg Kaiser and Ernst Toller were characterised by distorted and unrealistic performances during which the actors would move around the highly stylised sets in a jerky manner, shouting and gesturing broadly. The aim here was to express inner feelings in the most dramatic and extreme of ways. By the time then that Expressionism made its transition to cinema – a date traditionally marked by the release of Robert Wiene's *Das Cabinet des Dr. Caligari* in February 1920 – German audiences immediately recognised as familiar some of the characteristics that featured so prominently in the film.

1.4 THE STYLISTIC TRAITS OF EXPRESSIONIST CINEMA

What do we exactly think of when we think about Expressionist cinema? This question is less obvious than what it may appear at first because the very definition of Expressionist cinema has long been questioned and debated. A restricted definition would only include those films that followed the stylistic traits of *Das Cabinet des Dr. Caligari* and that preserved a close link to Expressionist theatre in their mise-en-scène. However, between 1920 and 1927 – the years that roughly bracket cinematic Expressionism – Germany produced and released about two dozen films that presented at least some of the features that can be retraced in Robert Wiene's film. This broader definition is certainly more useful and productive since it allows us to work on a much wider sample of works: film historian Kristin Thompson in her 1981 study on *Eisenstein's*

Ivan the Terrible proposes a definition of cinematic Expressionism that can encompass with a good degree of approximation all the possible stylistic variations falling under the Expressionist label. In her words then, Expressionism is:

> […] a general attempt to minimise the differences among the four aspects of *mise-en-scène*: lighting, costume, figure disposition and behaviour, and setting. The expressionist film makes, as much as possible, a single visual material of these aspects; the result is an emphasis on overall composition.[8]

If we then take 'composition' as the key defining word, it becomes easy to see that, despite diversified emphases and styles, all the films that can be regarded one way or another as Expressionist placed the utmost importance not so much on the editing aspect – that tended to be based on continuity and classic techniques such as crosscutting and shot/reverse shot – or on the camerawork – that although often employing extreme angles also made large use of straight-on and eye level shots – but on individual images that tried to blend the different elements into a sort of moving tableaux around which the eye of the spectator is free to roam in order to take in all of its composing elements. The sets – normally reconstructed in the studio but with some notable exceptions like *Nosferatu* – often merged with the actors thus creating a single compositional unit that was further enriched by the distinctive use of geometric elements such as lines and shapes – think for example of the recurrent arch motive employed by Murnau in *Nosferatu* or about the crooked and oppressive lines that constitute the preponderance of *Caligari*'s sets – and by the attention placed on *chiaroscuro* lighting that added another layer of distortion and exaggeration to the often nightmarish quality of these films. Costumes and the acting style were equally part of this wider approach to composition: when Conrad Veidt walks along the crooked sets of *Caligari* he becomes part of them. Likewise in *Nosferatu* the identification between the character of Count Orlok and his isolated lair is so ingrained in the narrative that the film's last image, after the vampire's death, is that of his solitary castle lying in ruins: the destruction of the Count's body translates directly into the destruction of his dwelling.

However, not all Expressionist films managed to achieve this ideal fusion of sets, lights, costumes and acting behaviour into a perfectly contained composition. Some film historians (see, for example, David Bordwell and Kristin Thompson) have underlined how this blend often only worked at intervals. The excessive emphasis on the single shot and on the creation of a tableau seamlessly blending the various elements inevitably clashed at times with the inner nature of the motion picture itself where movement – or, in other words, the advancement of the plot – is an essential part for the success of any narrative film. This contrast between mise-en-scène and narrative progression often caused the action to proceed very much like the actors on the set, in fits and jolting movements rather than in a smooth manner. Despite these alternating results, the films produced during the years of the Weimar Republic also tended to revolve around a common series of specific narrative concerns that reflected some troubling aspects of Weimar's public life and that were subsequently translated onto the screen in the various and differing ways we have just outlined. In his book on German Expressionism, Ian Roberts provides an overview of these thematic concerns by underlining for instance an interest in the depiction of the world as a liminal space between fantasy and reality and the frequent preference for stories focusing on a sense of threat towards individuals, couples, or society – just like the threat posed by Count Orlok in *Nosferatu* – two aspects that appear to be particularly important throughout the chronological arch of Weimar cinema. Other important themes – not directly touched in *Nosferatu* but equally important for an overall appreciation of German cinema of the 1920s – are the depiction of a dystopian futuristic society (e.g. Fritz Lang's *Metropolis*, 1927), an attention for stories inspired by traditional German folklore and mythology (e.g. *Die Nibelungen* again by Fritz Lang and realised in 1924), and, especially towards the end of the Weimar Republic, a focus on a more realistic depiction of society (e.g. G.W. Pabst's *Die Büchse der Pandora*, 1928).

CHAPTER 2 – BRINGING THE UNDEAD TO LIFE

2.1 THE FILM'S CREW

In line with the preferred working pattern of Weimar cinema that placed at its centre the so-called 'director-unit' – a system whereby each film was the product of a closely-knit collaboration of director, screenwriter, set designer, and cameraman – *Nosferatu* can be regarded not just as the product of the artistic genius of F. W. Murnau but also as the brainchild of at least three other men: the producer and set designer Albin Grau, the screenwriter Henrik Galeen, and, although to a somewhat lesser extent, the cameraman Fritz Arno Wagner. The first section of this chapter will provide a brief outline of their personalities and careers.

The film's producer and set designer was Albin Grau (1884-1971), an architect, artist and eminent occultist who claimed to have conceived the idea of a film on vampires after having an eerie conversation with a local peasant – whose own father had turned out to be a vampire – while being deployed on the front during the First World War. Grau wrote about this episode in an article for *Bühne und Film* in 1921 and its beginning seems to be the ideal set up of many a vampire story:

> It was during the winter of the war year 1916, in Serbia. […] The flickering flame of a slowly burning lamp threw phantasmatic shadows throughout the depths of the room that served as our billet. […] All of a sudden, one of my comrades […] cast into the darkness a portentous question. 'Do you know that we're all more or less tormented by vampires?' […] For a moment, there presided a deadly silence... […] It was then that from the darkest corner of the room the answer came. Frightened, we saw the old peasant make the sign of the cross - he came forward and […] he whispered to us: 'Before this wretched war, I was over in Romania. You can laugh about this superstition, but I swear on the mother of God, that I myself knew that horrible thing of seeing an undead.' - 'An undead?' one of us asked. - 'Yes, an undead or Nosferatu, as vampires are called over there. […] We've been pursued and tormented by those monsters forever.' Again he crossed himself. Then suddenly his voice grew hushed. 'One shouldn't speak of them at this hour,' he resumed, throwing a furtive glance toward the grandfather clock. We followed his gaze… Midnight! Our nerves had

grown extremely tense. We pressed him in a single voice: 'Tell us!' Today I'm still frozen by a shiver at the memory of that Serb's terrible story... [...][9]

The article then proceeds in providing the details of the old peasant's story – that is also accompanied by a lengthy quotation from an official document used to establish and support the reliability of the account. It is interesting though, how towards the end of the article, Grau also makes a sombre connection between vampires and the destruction brought on by the war. This is an aspect that, as we will see later, could be easily superimposed onto the film and used as a fruitful interpreting tool:

[...] Years passed. One no longer reads the terror of war in the eyes of men; but something of it has remained. Suffering and grief have weakened the heart of man and have bit by bit stirred up the desire to understand what is behind this monstrous event that is unleashed across the earth like a cosmic *vampire* to drink the blood of millions and millions of men...[10]

Grau was heavily involved in the world of German occultism and was a close associate of Heinrich Tränker, the inventor of 'Pansophism', a system of belief that put together elements of Rosicrucianism, Theosophy and Freemasonry. At the end of January 1921, in association with the businessman Enrico Dieckmann, Grau founded his production company and called it Prana Film, using a Sanskrit word roughly translatable as 'breath of life' and a symbol replicating the traditional yin and yang circle.

Despite its initial business plan to produce and release a total of nine films, which were all in one way or another connected with supernatural themes with titles such as *Hollenträume* (*Dreams of Hell*) and *Der Sumpfteufel* (*The Swamp Devil*), Prana Film, hit hard by the legal controversies triggered by the unauthorised adaptation of Bram Stoker's *Dracula* (the details of which will be discussed later on in this chapter) had to file for bankruptcy soon after the release of *Nosferatu* that thus remained the company's first and only film.

During the making of *Nosferatu*, Albin Grau was responsible for the sets, costumes and make-up and was also behind the mysterious and intriguing advertising campaign – of which the article quoted above is part – that preceded the film's release. Influenced by artists such as Henry Fuseli and Hugo Steiner-Prag, Grau experimented a little with

Figure 1 A design for the film by producer and set designer Albin Grau

the appearance of the vampire and produced a series of sketches that demonstrate how his visual concept ended up almost unchanged in the final version of the film.[11]

Grau even created the lettering of the inter-titles and the mysterious alphabet made up of occult symbols, letters and drawings used in the message exchanged between Count Orlok and the estate agent Knock that can be seen in a couple of rapid sequences of the film and that will be briefly discussed in the analytical chapter of this book. In one word, he was the man behind the scenes, the one who had first conceived and envisioned Count Orlok's world and had then brought Murnau on board to bring this world to life onto the screen.

The task of writing up the film's script was given to Henrik Galeen (1881-1949), a former journalist who had worked – just like Murnau – for the renowned theatre director Max Reinhardt before starting a career in cinema as screenwriter and director in 1913. Apart from his work on *Nosferatu*, Galeen should be remembered for at least other four important German films made between 1915 and 1928: *Der Golem* (*The Golem*, Henrik Galeen, 1915), *Das Wachsfigurenkabinett* (*Waxworks*, Paul Leni, 1924), *Der Student von Prag* (*The Student of Prague*, Henrik Galeen, 1926), and *Alraune* (*A Daughter of Destiny*, Henrik Galeen, 1928). Galeen produced his script for *Nosferatu* by following more or less the events of the original story – although he also inserted into the plot some significant alterations and simplifications that shall be discussed later on in this chapter. As pointed out by David J. Skal:

[…] Henrik Galeen […] faced with adapting a lenghty, rather wordy Victorian novel as a silent film, deftly excised everything except the visual, metaphorical, and mythic.[12]

The original script, reproduced by Lotte Eisner in her biography of Murnau, remains famous for its florid narrative style that sets it miles apart from what would nowadays be considered an acceptable film script. Eisner, introducing the script's translation in her book, describes it as a typical example of Expressionist writing

[characterised by] oddly broken lines, looks like blank verse […]. We [referring here to Eisner and translator Gertrud Mander] have followed the original in its prolific use of exclamation marks, words in capitals, and letter-spaced lower-case matter. Most noticeably, we have tried to keep the staccato rhythm of the original, with its incomplete sentences, clauses, phrases, and idiosyncratic punctuation; and we have avoided the temptation of grammatical tidiness or narrative smoothness.[13]

The task of filming under Murnau's direction was given to the UFA cameraman Fritz Arno Wagner (1889-1958) who is now widely regarded as one of the best German cinematographers – along with Karl Freund and Eugen Schüfftan – active between the 1920s and the 1950s. Wagner was a master in reproducing the dark, moody lighting that characterized the Expressionist movement, or as Lotte Eisner simply put it 'under Murnau's direction the camera of Fritz Arno Wagner required no extraneous factors to evoke the bizzarre'[14] and '[…] it was in the portrayal of horror that the camera of […] Fritz Arno Wagner excelled'.[15] *Nosferatu* probably remains Wagner's most famous work, it is worth remembering however that he did work with Murnau on other two films: *Schloss Vogelöd* (*The Haunted Castle*, 1921) and *Der brennende Acker* (*The Burning Soil*, 1922). Other notable collaborations were those with Ernst Lubitsch (*Madame Du Barry*, 1919), and Fritz Lang (*Der müde Tod* – *Between Two Worlds*, 1921; *Spione* – *Spies*, 1928; *M*, 1931; and *Das Testament des Dr. Mabuse* – *The Testament of Dr Mabuse*, 1933).

Of course, in the traditional director-unit, the guiding role and ultimate influence was reserved to the director himself and we know – for instance by reading his notes on the margins of Galeen's script – that Murnau was actively and heavily involved in all phases of pre-production and filmmaking. The heir of a family of textile manufacturers, Friedrich Wilhelm Plumpe (his real name) was born in Bielefeld (Westphalia) in 1888. From the stories recounted by members of his family and from the exhaustive biography published by Lotte Eisner in 1973, we know that he was a child and an adolescent prone to daydreaming and passionate about literature, theatre and art. As remembered by Murnau's brother, Robert Plumpe Murnau:

'[…] the dreams that seemed to weave around his being at night surrounded him by day as well. When we were out for a walk my mother used to have to keep saying to him: 'Look where you're going - you're dreaming again.'[16]

In 1907 Murnau moved to Berlin to study philology and soon after that he went to Heidelberg to read history of art and literature. In Heidelberg, his involvement with drama societies proved to be fateful for his future life and career for it was during a students' performance that Max Reinhardt spotted him and asked him to join his company, the Deutsches Theater. During his years as a student, Murnau developed a profound sentimental and almost certainly sexual relationship with a young poet, Hans Ehrenbaum Degele. It was through Hans, who came from a wealthy family of Jewish bankers and intellectuals, that the future director first got in touch with Berlin's bohemian underworld where he met and befriended, amongst others, the actor Conrad Veidt, the poet Else Lasker-Schüler, and the Expressionist painter Franz Marc. It was also during this period that Friedrich finally abandoned his family name in order to adopt the stage name of Murnau, an act that was at the same time an homage to the little artist' colony of Murnau am Staffelsee in the Upper Bavarian region where he had travelled with Hans and a gesture of defiance towards his father who strongly opposed Friedrich's artistic ambitions. In 1914, Murnau joined the ranks of the German army to fight in the First World War. His experience during the conflict – first in the infantry and then in the Luftwaffe – was profoundly marked by the death of Hans who was killed in action while deployed on the Russian front in July 1915. The American novelist Jim Shepard in his fictionalised but extensively researched account of Murnau's life (*Nosferatu in Love*, published in 1998) imagines a Murnau so haunted and obsessed by Hans' death that all his subsequent work can be read as a mournful reflection on love and loss.

Hans was the anguish that pulled its plow through his sleep. After six years, Murnau
was still a house in which the largest room was sealed.[17]

Murnau's life as a Luftwaffe reconnaissance pilot – an experience that probably had
an influence on his subsequent camerawork style – was cut short in 1917 when his
airplane got lost in the fog and he was forced to make an emergency landing in the
neutral territory of Switzerland. Murnau awaited the end of the hostilities as a prisoner
of war in an internment camp in Andermatt where he kept himself busy with amateur
theatre performances. In 1919, back in Germany after the armistice, Murnau moved into
Hans' family house – Hans' mother, the opera singer Mary Ehrenbaum Degele explicitly
wished for him to do so in her will – and after setting up a production company with
Conrad Veidt, he produced his first eight feature films. After the completion of *Nosferatu*,
Murnau continued to work in Germany until 1926 directing amongst other films *Der
letze Mann* (*The Last Laugh*, 1924) and an adaptation of Goethe's Faust (1926) and
then moved to the United States where he would work on four more films. In 1927
he directed his only American success, *Sunrise: a Song of Two Humans*. In 1931, along
with documentary filmmaker Robert J. Flaherty, Murnau travelled to Bora Bora to film
what would turn out to be his last film, *Tabu*. Back in the United States for the official
premiere of the film – that, due to artistic differences with Flaherty, he had completed
on his own – the director died tragically in a car crash on the Pacific Coast Highway on
the 11th of March 1931. The circumstances of his death created all sorts of rumours
within the Hollywood community: Murnau was said to be fascinated by Eastern
philosophy, astrology and occultism and on the day of his death he was going to arrange
a steamship journey to New York after having been warned not to travel by land. As
underlined by Thomas Elsaesser in his study of Weimar cinema:

> Whether part of the Murnau legend or authentic, the accounts of the circumstances
> of his death are a strangely apt tribute to his aura. It seals his life with a melancholy
> gesture of mysterious irony, not unlike that emanating from his films.[18]

2.2 PRODUCTION AND RECEPTION

After completing the film's casting – that saw Max Schreck (Count Orlok), Gustav von Wangenheim (Hutter), Greta Schroeder (Ellen), and Alexander Granach (Knock) in the four main roles – Murnau and his crew started shooting *Nosferatu*. The filming commenced in August 1921 and lasted until October. It is interesting to notice how, unlike the vast majority of Expressionist films, *Nosferatu* was mostly filmed on location and the crew travelled extensively between Germany, the former Czechoslovakia and Poland in order to shoot sequences in the Baltic ports of Rostock, Wismar and Lübeck whilst the interiors were shot in Berlin in the Jofa-Atelier studios. In the early 1920s, filming on location was still somewhat of a novelty but it was certainly cheaper than reconsructing sets in studios. In the case of *Nosferatu* it is quite likely that the decision of filming on location was not simply an artistic one but was also connected to the company's budget limitations. Throughout the production period, the audience's curiosity was awakened and maintained alive by the constant release of adverts, posters and articles that Albin Grau cleverly circulated and published in various film magazines such as *Der Film*, and *Bühne und Film*. For instance, a reader buying issue number 21 of *Bühne und Film* (1921) would find – along with the above-mentioned article on vampires written by Albin Grau and a number of posters and sketches – the following publicity that openly challenged the public to be brave enough to face Prana's first feature film:

A million fancies strike you when you hear the name: Nosferatu!

NOSFERATU

does not die!

What do you expect of the first showing of this great work?

Aren't you afraid? - Men must die. But legend has it that a vampire, *Nosferatu*, Ôder Untote (the Undead), lives on men's blood! You want to see a symphony of horror? You may expect more. Be careful. *Nosferatu* is not just fun, not something to be taken lightly. Once more: beware.[19]

In order to further increase the buzz around the film, journalists were at times invited on the Berlin set to observe and report on the work in progress. The publicity created by Prana Film reached its climax on the 4th of March 1922 when *Nosferatu* finally had its premiere in the Marble Hall of the Berlin Zoological Gardens. The decision to present the film at the zoo rather than in a place more in tune with a Gothic tale such as a church seems to suggest how, in the minds of its authors, *Nosferatu* could be regarded as an observation of nature – albeit a nature inhabited by vampires and supernatural beings – and not a purely Gothic fantasy. On March 3rd the *Film Kurier* anticipated that Prana Film had arranged a party 'in true American style' for the launch of their latest film. Starting at eight o'clock, the party was expected to last all night long and to occupy 'the entire premises of the zoo'. The guests, although not required to do so, were invited to attend wearing Biedermeier costumes.[20] A couple of days after the premiere, Alfred Rosenthal wrote a lengthy piece for the special Monday edition of the *Berlin Lokal-Anzeiger*. Rosenthal reported on the spooky atmosphere surrounding the film's screening – '[…] the room darkened as the projectors began to whir and a title annouced that a symphony of horror should roll across the screen […]' – and commented with more than a hint of irony upon the celebrities who turned up for the film and the following lavish ball:

'[…] the Symphony of Horror degenerated into a ball. One could see the celebrities of the cinema world: Lubitsch, Kräly, Johannes Riemann, Heinz Schall, the large distributors, film stars and those who believed to be one.'[21]

Overall, as reported by the *Film Kurier*, the lauch of the film was a highly successful affair and '[…] the guests quickly turned the "symphony of horror and darkness" into a delightful "symphony of joy and light"'.[22]

The generally favourable reactions to the film were counterbalanced by a rather venomous article which appeared in the Marxist newspaper *Leipziger Volkzeitunger* soon after the premiere. The article accused *Nosferatu* of enveloping the worker in a 'supernatural fog' that would masquerade and hide concrete reality with the result of sapping the working class' revolutionary drive. This numbing 'supernatural fog' was a direct consequence of the spiritualist revival – that was secretly steered by the world of finance and industry – that had stormed Europe and America right after the end of the war when people would try to find comfort to the inconceivable grief caused by the conflict by resorting to any available means. Marxists regarded spiritualism as yet another form of opiate for the masses – just like traditional religion – and *Nosferatu* appeared to be part of this wider conspiracy that aimed at keeping 'people sufficiently stupid for capitalist interests.'[23] The only possible reaction would be

[…] not to give […] money to a cinema that is going to show […] a propaganda film, financed by industry and intended to deaden […] minds. [This way] the whole pretty plan will fail, and the phantom *Nosferatu* can well let himself be devoured by his own rats.[24]

What none of these articles reported, though, was the fact that the launch of the film had cost Prana more than the feature itself and that the whole project had been realised without obtaining the necessary legal permissions from whoever owned the rights to *Dracula* – a detail that no one had worried about in the pre-production stage perhaps even thinking that applying some cosmetic adjustments to the plot - such as anticipating the story to the beginning of the nineteenth century and changing the characters' names – would be enough to keep the film safe from all possible issues. These facts confirm that impression of impracticality and lack of any real business sense that seemed to surround all of the initiatives undertaken by Prana Film during its brief commercial life – and on the long run they also proved to be fatal for the very survival of the company that was now about to encounter its fiercest adversary in the elderly widow of Bram Stoker.

2.3 CONTROVERSY AND LEGAL ACTION

At the end of April 1922, Florence Stoker, the sixty-four years old widow of the Irish writer, received a series of documents from Germany that included the programme and some promotional material for a film premiere that had taken place in Berlin's Zoological Gardens at the beginning of the previous month. The film advertised in the programme – 'frei verfaßt von [freely adapted by] Henrik Galeen' – was obviously *Nosferatu*, a feature about which Florence Stoker – who partly survived on the unsteady income provided by *Dracula*'s rights – did not know anything at all since no one from Prana Film had neither thought about asking for her permission nor had considered paying her for the adaptation rights to the story. Outraged and upset, the woman turned to the British Incorporated Society of Authors, which she had joined only a few days before, right after having discovered the film's existence, for protection and legal advice. After filing a lawsuit against Prana Film, Florence Stoker's lawyers asked for compensation for the illegal use of intellectual property. The legal battle between the widow and Prana Film would drag on for over three years - and would cause a considerable series of headaches even to the Society of Authors whose secretary, G.

Herbert Thring, was literally stalked and harassed by Florence Stoker who still had many influential friends within London's literary and editorial circles. In May 1922, the Society of Authors surrendered to her pressures and asked its legal representative in Germany – Dr. Wronker-Flatow – to follow the matter with the caveat that should Prana Film wished to fight against the case, the Society would not assist Florence Stoker in taking the question any further. Still unbeknownst to Thring, this initial intention was never really carried through due to Florence Stoker's fierce determination and single-mindedness in pursuing her German 'foes'. In June 1922, Prana, whose already precarious finances had been hit hard by the initial legal costs caused by the lawsuit and in order to avoid having to pay even more money, filed for bankruptcy. Meanwhile *Nosferatu* was still being screened in cinemas around Germany and Hungary and in August the legal representative of the production company proposed a compromise to Florence Stoker. She would receive a share in the film's profits in exchange for the use of the name *Dracula* in the English and American markets. Stoker's widow refused to accept the deal and then spent the following two years (1923 and 1924) insisting with the Society of Authors that her case should be taken seriously for principles of both fairness and law. Realising that it was rather unlikely to succeed in obtaining any financial compensation from Prana, she also started demanding the destruction of all the existing copies of *Nosferatu* – a film she had never even seen – both negative and positive ones. Eventually, on 20th July 1925, a Berlin court ruled that Prana Film was indeed guilty of copyright infringement and, since the company could not meet any monetary reparations, the court ordered to destroy the film. As underlined by David J. Skal in his detailed account of the legal controversy between Prana Film and Florence Stoker,

> No doubt […] the story will […] horrify film conservators and historians […]. Most 'lost' films have vanished through neglect. But in the case of *Nosferatu* we have one of the few instances in film history, and perhaps the only one, in which an obliterating capital punishment is sought for a work of cinematic art, strictly on legalistic ground, by a person with no knowledge of the work's specific contents or artistic merit.[25]

Florence Stoker's victory over Count Orlok was only a fleeting and apparent one. The German court did not provide any concrete evidence of the film's obliteration and, although the original negative never resurfaced, *Nosferatu* reappeared almost immediately in England where, under the title of 'Dracula', it was advertised as part of the showings of a newly-formed British Film Society. Yet again, following the advice of the Society of Authors, Florence Stoker sent a registered letter to the people organising the screenings forbidding any showing of the film anywhere, anytime, and under any circumstances. Even this latest legal act was not enough, though, for the film kept on being offered to cinemas around Britain – with no-one ever being able to locate who was responsible for its diffusion. Finally, after quietly laying dormant for a few short years awaiting for the right chance to rise again, the film resurfaced in the summer of 1929 in the United States where it was advertised for a series of screenings in Detroit and in New York City where it opened at the Film Guild Cinema in the Greenwich Village from where it started once again its unstoppable voyage through space and time.

It is important to notice that, despite its difficult survival, *Nosferatu* was never really a lost film and there were various copies appearing and disappearing around Europe and the United States. For example, Henri Langlois, director of the Cinémathèque Française in Paris, preserved a copy of the second version of the film dated 1926 or 1927. A print from this version – that was in black and white and not with the original tones and tints – travelled to the Museum of Modern Art in New York in 1947 where its intertitles were translated into English and the names of the characters were changed to those in the novel. This was also the version that returned to Europe and was presented around in the 1960s as a prime example of Weimar cinema that by then was going through a phase of rediscovery and reevaluation. According to the necessities of the various screenings, the film's intertitles were translated from language to language and with each new copy the deterioration in the image quality became consistent. To further add to the confusion, in 1930, a 'second' *Nosferatu* also appeared on the market: it was called *Die zwölfte Stunde* (*The Twelfth Hour*) and was advertised as an 'artistic adaptation' of the story by a certain Dr. Waldemar Roger. The film was intended to be released with the accompaniment of sound recorded on a grammophone record and contained additions, shortened sections, additional characters, sequences moved from one part of the film to another and even a happy ending. It is almost entirely thanks to Lotte Eisner's efforts if today we can watch the film as it was intended to be. In the 1950s she managed to obtain the original script of the film from Murnau's brother, Robert Plumpe. The script, as we know, presented a series of alterations to Galeen's original which were handwritten by the director himself and it was used as a blueprint against the copy held at the Cinémathèque Française and other versions of the film. In this way, restorators and film scholars such as Enno Patalas and Luciano Berriatúa, managed to reconstruct an Ur version of the film that was subsequently completed with the original subtitles and colours.

2.4 FROM THE PAGE TO THE SCREEN

Leaving aside all the legal controversies, how similar *Nosferatu* really was to its literary source?

In we attempt to compare and contrast the two, it becomes immediately apparent that Murnau's film preserved the basic plot of the story (a young man travels to an isolated area to sell a house to a mysterious count / the count turns out to be a vampire who travels back to the young man's town bringing death and destruction with him / the vampire is destroyed at the end of the story) whilst at the same time implementing a series of important changes both in terms of micro details and from a wider narrative perspective.

One of the most interesting features of *Dracula* is its epistolary structure – the story is not recounted by one narrator but builds up through a series of diary entries, letters, phonographic recordings, newspapers clippings et cetera by means of which the characters relate their experiences to the readers. The multiple documents that constitute *Dracula*'s narrative peculiarity also imply that the story is constantly reconstructed and retold from a series of different points of view: each character, except from Count Dracula himself, contributes with his/her own segment of the story and it is up to the reader, and to Mina Harker in the second part of the novel, to try and piece things together in a coherent and cohesive way.

Nosferatu attempts to replicate some aspects of the novel's epistolary structure by introducing five different voices into the action. The film opens up with the pages of a book whose narrator proclaims to be the historical chronicle of the events that took place in the town of Wisborg during the plague epidemic of 1838. This unnamed narrator will appear again throughout the film to clarify, explain and interpret some of the events taking place on the screen. His perspective is removed from the story for we know he did not take part in the events narrated, but time and again, he reports or recalls conversations he had with the surviving protagonists of the plague, such as Hutter, thus providing the story with a degree of authenticity and reliability. The other voices inserted in the film have a very similar role: the entries from the ship's log bringing Orlok to Wisborg increase our belief in the terrifying events taking place on the schooner during its dramatic journey; the newspaper's cutting chronicling the spreading of the plague in Transylvania and along the Black Sea ports purports to report real events and increases at the same time the tension connected to the inevitable tragedy that is approaching by sea. Even the *Book of Vampires* – detailing the nature and main features of the vampire – grounds the monster and the events surrounding him in a concrete reality and not in an imaginary dimension. Finally, the glimpses we get of the letters sent by Hutter to his wife provide us with a window into their intimate relationship and into Hutter's lack of immediate understanding of what is going on around him.

The similarities in the narrative structure are also counterbalanced by a series of differences, the most obvious and visible of them being the change in the time and place of the story – apart from the parts set in Transylvania that are present both in the book and the film, the novel takes place in London in 1897 while the film is set in the fictional town of Wisborg, a sort of idealised middle-European town, in 1838. These modifications could simply be interpreted as a somewhat clumsy attempt on the part of the filmmakers to distantiate their film enough from its source novel so as to avoid possible copyright problem. Even if the people at Prana Film did not know about the existence of Florence Stoker – and it is rather likely that they did not – the novel was still in print (and so it has remained since its first publication), and it is therefore reasonable to imagine that the copyright issue must have been somewhere in the mind of Grau and his associates. It is important to consider though how these changes also triggered in the film a series of consequences that are worth underlining.

As pointed out by Martin Tropp, Stoker's novel belongs to a type of fiction in which 'an unusual individual in touch with private fears at a time when these fears were shared by the outside world consciously or unconsciously exploited the link between the two.'[26] *Dracula* is therefore a novel steeped in late-Victorian London and the proximity to the new century with its social and technological innovations plays an important part in the book both in terms of form and content. Technology is utilised and presented by Stoker under various forms and circumstances: Mina employs a typewriter to put together the different testimonies that will help the hunters to track Dracula down, Dr. Seward makes recordings of his conversations with Renfield, Van Helsing tries to save Lucy's life by means of blood transfusions etc. These episodes though are not merely accidentals but contribute to increase the insurmountable distance between the evil world of Dracula, which is centuries old and frozen in the limbo of his non-death, and the modern world of the novel's heroes who can turn to science and modern means of trasportation such as the train to eventually overcome their enemy.

In the film, bringing back the time of the action to the early nineteenth century and more specifically to the Biedermeier era, makes the gap between the modern world and that inhabited by the vampire much smaller and harder to notice, so much so that the rural world of the Transylvanian peasants does not appear too different after all from the one inhabited by Hutter and Ellen. If in *Dracula* religion and folklore are accompanied by science, in *Nosferatu* the vampire is destroyed by ancient atavistic forces such as purity and the rays of the sun.

The shift from modernity to the Biedermeier period could also be read as a subtle attempt on the part of Murnau to comment on the stifling state of contemporary German society without raising the question directly and in a way that could result to be too controversial. The Biedermeier period (which can be roughly bracketed between the years 1815 and 1848) coincided with the rise of a new middle-class whose success was boosted by industrial progress and with a generalised lack of political commitment in the arts that was the direct result of the growing climate of political oppression widespread in Europe after the end of the Napoleonic wars. The inward tendencies of the era when combined with the desire of the new bourgeousie to show off its newly acquired wealth, resulted in an increased interest and development in the field of interior design. Biedermeier décor – that had been rediscovered in 1906 at the Centennial Exhibition of the National Gallery in Berlin – was basically a toned down version of the boastful and rich Empire style and was characterised by a rather reliable, common sense and somewhat boring idea of space and furniture. By setting his film in this specific cultural and visual climate – and by often enclosing his heroine within the confined space of her well-appointed bourgeois house – Murnau underlines the sense of oppression and seclusion experienced by marginalised sections of society, such as women and possibly by extension also homosexuals.

Another notable adaptation feature of Murnau's film can be identified in the change in the characters' names and also in the drastic reduction of their number and function. The role of some characters thus results to be much more limited than in the source novel; for instance, Renfield, the estate agent who is sent to Transylvania before Jonathan Harker only to come back from his journey deranged and under the spell of the vampire for whom he acts as a sort of minion, is partially replaced in the film by Knock who also fills in the narrative role of Harker's employer. Other characters instead, have been simply obliterated from the film's narrative. There is no trace therefore of Dracula's hunters, Quincey Morris, Dr. Seward and Arthur Holmwood. If *Dracula* is a choral book, then, *Nosferatu* really revolves around its three main characters: Hutter, Ellen and Count Orlok.

Hutter – Jonathan Harker in the novel – is portrayed as a brave man in love with his wife who ultimately lacks the necessary degree of empathy and sensitivity to understand her dramatic internal turmoil. His perspective on the events often appears to be rather short-sighted, his energy – especially at the beginning of the film Murnau frequently films Gustav von Wangenheim running or striding briskly through the frame – is made up of short bursts but has no real stamina and more than once during the confrontation with the vampire he becomes passive and ineffectual. For example, when he is attacked by the vampire during his second night at the castle he retreats under his bedcovers like a child and when he discovers the body of the Count asleep in his coffin, instead of attempting to destroy him while he is at his weakest, Hutter runs away in a mad panic. These shortcomings in his personality will make him ultimately incapable of preventing Ellen's death.

The female heroine in *Nosferatu* is portrayed in an elusive and subtle way constantly oscillating between passivity and action. Mina, Ellen's literary counterpart, is a modern Victorian woman: although not a 'New Woman' in the purest sense of the word and somewhat conventional in her outlook on life, she nevertheless has a job and knows how to use technology – it is thanks to her proficiency in using a typewriter that Dracula's movements are reconstructed and the vampire is finally killed – and her character is fashioned as a combination of traditional feminine warmth and masculine determination. As Van Helsing declares in Chapter XVIII of the novel: 'Ah, that wonderful Madam Mina! She has man's brain – a brain that a man should have were he much gifted – and a woman's heart.'[27] Compared to Mina, Ellen is harder to understand. The first time we see her, she is playing joyfully with a kitten and could at first appear as a rather carefree and even childish character. However, this superficial impression is soon dispelled by what can be interpreted as Ellen's deep affinity with nature: there are many instances in the film when this aspect becomes clear – see, for example, her reaction in the sequence where she is presented with a posy of flowers by Hutter that will be discussed in the close reading chapter of this book. If Hutter is filmed running about the set, Ellen is often framed in a static situation, embroidering at the window or sitting on a solitary bench on the beach. Yet, her constant proximity to open spaces, such as the window and the sea, seems to suggest the possibility, and perhaps even the desire, for an escape into a different reality to which she seems to be already alert on a deeper and metaphysical level, as demonstrated for instance by those episodes in the film when Ellen 'feels' that Hutter is in danger in Orlok's castle and she reacts by sleepwalking or crying out for help while in a state of trance. When compared to Mina Harker, who eventually survives her encounter with the vampire – or, more precisely, is saved from the vampire by the men surrounding and protecting her – Ellen is also a much more tragic and solitary heroine whose faith almost coincides with that of martyrs. Her death is not caused by weakness but it is rather an act of supreme self-sacrifice – and also of self-assertion – which is first thought out and then carried through entirely on her own will and means and with no help from her husband or any other man who may surround her. As underlined by Matthew C. Brennan:

> Murnau makes Jonathan Harker's wife, Nina, the sole character capable of integrating the conscious and unconscious parts of the Self. [...] Nina's awareness of the vampire empowers her both to achieve psychic integrity and to serve as the sole avenger and savior of society.[28]

The formidable adversary that Ellen and Hutter have to face is an intriguing combination of elements taken from the novel, original diversions from it, and features pertaining to the folkloric depiction of vampires. In the second chapter of the book, Jonathan Harker povides a very detailed description of the Count:

His face was strong - a very strong - aquiline, with high bridge of the thin nose and peculiarly arched nostrils; with lofty domed forehead, and hair growing scantily round the temples, but profusely elsewhere. His eyebrows were very massive, almost meeting over the nose […] The mouth, so far as I could see it under the heavy moustache, was fixed and rather cruel-looking, with peculiarly sharp white teeth; [which] protruded over the lips […] For the rest, his ears were pale and at the tops extremely pointed; the chin was broad and strong, and the cheeks firm though thin. The general effect was one of extraordinary pallor.[29]

Murnau retained some elements of this description: his vampire is characterised by a strong aquiline profile, with a very wide forehead, bushy eyebrows and incredibly pointed ears. The extreme pallor is also maintained and is emphasised by the long black coat with tight lines constantly worn by Orlok that also seems to stress the unnatural thinness and height of the Count. Orlok's vampire's fangs though do not protrude over his lips and when we finally get to see them there is an immediate visual connection with rodents' teeth. Overall, we get the impression of a character that is 'more spectral, dried-out and leech-like' than the magnetic and sexually alluring counts portrayed by other successive on-screen vampires such as Bela Lugosi, Christopher Lee, and Gary Oldman.[30] Despite Count Orlok's hideous appearance, Murnau's vampire is not entirely devoid of a certain animalistic allure that can be retraced in Ellen's obsession for him and in a number of shots towards the end of the film when she is waiting for the vampire's arrival or when she finally meets him – in her conjugal bed – and her reaction to his shadow clutching her heart can be interpreted as a subtle combination of pain and sexual pleasure.

The ultimate faith of the vampire is another central difference between the film and the book. In *Dracula*, the Count escapes from London but is chased back to Transylvania by the collective effort of Van Helsing, Harker, Holmwood, Seward, Morris, and Mina and this pursuit constitutes one of the most exciting and breathtaking parts of the book. Once cornered outside his castle, Dracula is then dispatched by Jonathan Harker and Quincey Morris – who will be the only human casualty in this last part of the book – who slash his throat and stab him through the heart. Stoker provides his readers with a neat closure: the Count's body crumbles to ashes and order is restored – in a coda set seven years after the events we see Mina and Jonathan bringing up their son Quincey, and Seward and Holmwood being happily married. Murnau is not so generous with his audience: the film does not have any major climatic scene. There is no investigative work or collective effort involved in dispatching the vampire but rather a sombre sense of sacrifice and inevitability. Even the very death of the vampire, who simply disappears into a thin puff of smoke when hit by the sunlight coming in from Ellen's window, appears to be strangely anti-climatic in its rapid deployment. There is closure – after all the vampire is dead – but no real sense of resolution and certainly no happy ending to the story. Interestingly though, the closing sequence in *Nosferatu* will establish a central convention of the vampiric genre: in *Dracula* the vampire is weakened during the day but does not fear the direct light of the sun and it is with Murnau's film that this famous topos begins. Besides, as underlined by Anne Billson:

> Films, like vampires, thrive on darkness. To see a filmed image you have to shut out the sunlight and cast your surroundings into night, so it's fitting that cinema's first major addition to the vampire playbook should be the creature's vulnerability to daylight […] when […] Graf Orlok fades into nothingness at the end of F.W. Murnau's 1922 film […] Light became as important as stakes and holy water in the vampire-hunter's arsenal.[31]

In terms of characters whose role and importance have either been reduced or modified in the film, the two most interesting examples are those of Professor Van Helsing and Lucy Westenra. In Stoker's novel, Count Dracula finds his fiercest adversary and nemesis in the character of Professor Abraham Van Helsing, an energetic and resolute Dutchman who combines scientific knowledge – we know he is a Doctor of Medicine, Philosophy, Letters, and Law – with less orthodox methods, such as magic and folklore. Van Helsing is constructed by Stoker to be the real hero in the novel (he even shares his name with the author) and he is the only character truly capable of destroying Dracula and save Mina and by extension the rest of mankind. Once introduced in the story, by means of a lengthy description in Mina's journal that can only be compared for its centrality in the book to Jonathan Harker's description of the Count, he immediately assumes total command in the battle against the vampire. As underlined by Clive Leatherdale, Van Helsing is a 'scientist-turned-magician' who is also at the same time a staunch upholder of the strictest moral values predicated by Roman Catholicism and an opponent of materialist bourgeois values and lax moral behaviour.[32] Despite his frequent lack of tact and conservative attitudes, though, Van Helsing is undeniably a formidable character to whom his cinematographic counterpart, Professor Bulwer, can hardly be a match. In Murnau's film, Bulwer is a scientist and a Paracelsian — as it will be clarified in a late sequence in the film where he is shown lecturing a small class of students — and his knowledge should therefore be an inextricable mixture of science and occultism. However, although knowledgeable, Bulwer is ultimately ineffectual and he never gets really involved in the fight against the vampire. It even remains unclear in the story whether he has any grasp or understanding of what is really going on in Wisborg and the film's closing shot presents him as an old and defeated man shaking his head in disbelief when confronted with Ellen's sudden and tragic death.

Another character whose importance and role have been modified and diminished in Murnau's adaptation is that of Mina's friend: Lucy Westenra. In the novel, the character of Lucy is put into sharp contrast with that of Mina: her flirtatious attitude and implied curiosity towards sex — along with her tendency to sleepwalk at night, a trait that is significantly attributed to Ellen in the film — seem to be crucial flaws in her personality and also the determining reasons in the fact that Dracula chooses her as his first victim in London. After her death, Lucy turns into an eroticised vampire — the 'Bloofer Lady' — who preys on little children at night, and is dispatched by Van Helsing and the other male characters in the most brutal and gruesome sequence of the novel. When she is ambushed in the chapel where she should be lying dead, Stoker describes her as a white figure characterised by

> [...] voluptuous wantonness [...] with lips [...] crimson with fresh blood [and] eyes unclean and full of hell-fire.[33]

Seeing her fiancée, Arthur Holmwood, with the others, she tries to lure him towards her by exercising her newly acquired lack of sexual inhibition:

> '[...] with a languorous, voluptuous grace [she] said: - "Come to me, Arthur. Leave these others and come to me. My arms are hungry for you. Come, and we can rest together. Come, my husband, come!"'[34]

After this unsettling encounter, it will be up to Arthur 'the husband' to bring Lucy's death to a real completion and to restore her '[...] as a holy, and not an unholy, memory' through an act that scholars have normally interpreted as a travesty for sexual intercourse.[35] Stoker is here pretty heavy-handed with his imagery:

> Arthur took the stake and hammer [...] Then he struck with all his might. The Thing in the coffin writhed; and a hideous, blood-curling screech came from the opened red lips. The body shook and quivered and twisted in wild contortions; [Arthur's] untrembling arm rose and fell, driving deeper and deeper the mercy-bearing stake [...] And then the writhing and quivering of the body became less [...] Finally it lay still. [...] The hammer fell from Arthur's hand. [...] The great drops of sweat sprang from his forehead, and his breath came in broken gasps.[36]

In Murnau's film, Lucy's character is replaced by that of Anny, the sister of the shipbuilder Harding who offers hospitality to Ellen while Hutter is away in Transylvania. Compared to Lucy, the film's character comes across as being pretty bland and insignificant. Although it is interesting to see her interact with Ellen and observe the contrast between Ellen's mournful countenance and Anny's youthful joy, the overall impression is that left by an accidental character who falls victim to the vampire just like many other innocent Wisborg citizens. If Lucy's death is a pivotal narrative moment in *Dracula* and is imbued by a rich subtext feeding from Victorian attitudes towards sex and fears of the new and independent woman on the rise, Anny's passing is treated by Murnau in an extremely understated, although poetic, way, with the fragile flickering flame of a candle being extinguished by a mysterious wind stirring the curtains of her bedroom.

Despite these changes and differences, *Nosferatu* arguably remains one of the most haunting and terrifying renditions of Bram Stoker's novel. The next chapter of the book will attempt to provide a close reading of the film using Noel Carroll's theory of the 'complex discovery plot' as a template and framework.

CHAPTER 3 – READING THE VAMPIRE

3.1 THE FILM ON DVD

Before moving on to a detailed analysis of *Nosferatu*, I would like to clarify that for the purposes of this book, all references and quotations of dialogue (both in German and English) will refer to the two DVD editions of the film released respectively by the British Film Institute in 2002 and by Eureka/Masters of Cinema in 2007. Although there are other versions of the film available on the market that tend to vary quite a lot in terms of quality and respect to the original film, these two releases present a number of important features that are worth mentioning here, such as the restoration of the original tints and colours, and the re-implementation of Albin Grau's intertitles. For what concerns the music in the case of the BFI, the film is accompanied by a newly composed soundtrack, whilst the Eureka edition features the first recorded rendition of the original score by Hans Erdmann.

The BFI version was restored in 1997 by the *Münchner Filmmuseum* and by the *Cineteca del Comune di Bologna*, whereas the version released by Eureka Film was restored by Luciano Berriatúa on behalf of the Friedrich-Wilhelm-Murnau-Stiftung in 2005/2006. More specifically, this edition employed a tinted nitrate print with French intertitles dated 1922 and preserved at the Cinémathèque Française as the basis for the restoration. The final product is the result of a long and complex work of investigation and reconstruction: some missing shots were retrieved using a 1939 safety print of the film preserved at the Bundesarchiv-Filmarchiv in Berlin/Koblenz, that was drawn from a Czech export print dating back to the 1920s. Other missing parts were instead taken from a nitrate print of 1930 that had been distributed under the title of *Die zwölfte Stunde* [*The Twelfth Hour*] and that was preserved at the Cinémathèque Française in Paris. Equally, the restoration and subsequent re-implementation of the original intertitles were based on another safety print dated 1962 and preserved in Berlin's Bunderarchiv/Filmarchiv that had as its basis a film's print made in 1922. The missing intertitles were redesigned before insertion and can be recognised in the Eureka print because they are marked 'FWMS' (Friedrich-Wilhelm-Murnau-Stiftung) at the bottom left corner of the screen.

Both versions replicate the tones and tints revealed by the surviving nitrate copy of the film thus giving the viewers the chance to truly appreciate the various narrative phases and nuances in the story that get inevitably lost in those purely black and white versions of the film where even Nosferatu's final demise through the first ray of the morning sun does not make any real visual narrative sense. In silent cinema, tints and colours were determined by a set of clear colour-codes; thus for instance, night scenes that have no other visible source of light apart from the moon are tinted in blue whilst interior sequences set during the day are tinted in an amber shade.

These two versions also utilise the original intertitles characterised by the lettering designed by the film's producer and set designer Albin Grau that recall closely the film's original script by Henrik Galeen.

The BFI edition also features a new orchestral score composed by James Bernard (1925-2001) that, through the combination and juxtaposition of several contrasting musical themes, reconnects the soundtrack to the idea of the film as a 'symphony' where visual and narrative elements combine with socio-political issues which were relevant to Germany in the 1920s such as anti-Semitism, racism, pan-Germanism, fear of homosexuality and the collapse of moral and social values. More specifically, James Bernard, who also composed the music for a number of Hammer films such as Terence Fisher's *Horror of Dracula* (1958), employs a series of very recognisable themes that although generally based on the bipolarity between Good and Evil, identified here by corresponding concordant and discordant sounds, accompany the various characters throughout the film. Therefore the three main characters are assigned their own musical theme, or to use the correct musical term – a leitmotif which the viewer can immediately recognise. Orlok's theme is based on the syllables *No-sfe-ra-tu* expressed as a four-note motif (along the lines of Bernard's work on the Dracula theme which was based on the Count's three-syllables name – *Dra-cu-la*) that is played by low heavy brass (four trumpets, four trombones and a tuba). The musical theme of the film's heroine Ellen, played by a large string section, conveys a sense of melancholy and romanticism but it is at the same time, intertwined with a secondary motif that subtly stresses the uncanny psychological link that runs between Ellen and the Count and that is established, as we will see, a number of times by Murnau by an artful use of editing and cross-cutting. Finally, Hutter's theme is the combination of two distinct motifs that are representative of the character's narrative evolution – although this evolution is never really accompanied by an equally profound development in the character's understanding of the plague or of his own wife's internal turmoil and intentions. The first theme, bouncy and lively, is played by woodwind instruments and is reminiscent of a rustic folk tune. It exemplifies Hutter's naivety and almost adolescent enthusiasm in undertaking his journey to the mysterious 'land of ghosts' where Orlok is waiting for him. This theme is almost imperceptibly replaced by a second, more obscure motif that Bernard based on the lower line of Nosferatu's own melodic tune. Hutter's and Nosferatu's life become inextricably linked as soon as Hutter crosses the castle's archway entrance and thus the same must happen to the themes identifying the two characters. Finally, the theme connected to the shady character of Knock, based on strings and percussion, is particularly effective during the chase scene towards the climax of the film when the inhabitants of Wisborg pursue Orlok's servant around the town and in the fields. The frantic and relentlessly fast pace of this sequence conveys in a very dramatic manner the desperation of the people battered by the mysterious plague that is decimating the town's inhabitants and their almost animalistic instinct towards revenge. Often combining melodic lines pertaining to different characters in one multi-layered theme, James Bernard's score manages to reproduce on an aural level the idea of the film as a symphony of converging narrative and thematic concerns.

The soundtrack on the Eureka edition is noteworthy because it features the original score composed for *Nosferatu* by the conductor, composer and music critic Hans Erdmann (1882-1942) in the reconstruction made by Berndt Heller. Erdmann gave his work the title *Fantastisch-Romantische Suite* which he divided into ten parts and was arranged in versions for both full and palm court orchestra (a term that indicates a smaller ensemble). Compared to the score by James Bernard, which follows the musical style of many of the Hammer film soundtracks, the original score by Erdmann is very much of its time, recalling the late German and Austrian romantic style. Composers such as Gustav Mahler, Richard Strauss and Alexander Zemlinsky particularly come to mind. Again, leitmotif is used but what this score really achieves very successfully is the expression of a wide range of emotion and characterisation. Other music is also included in the score: works by Bizet, Becce, Verdi, Boito and Percy E. Fletcher. The music for the closing sequence uses an orchestration of Chopin's *Nocturne in G minor, Op. 15/3*.

3.2 READING *NOSFERATU* AS A 'COMPLEX DISCOVERY PLOT'

In his book *The Philosophy of Horror* (1990), Noel Carroll identifies a generic narrative template structured around four phases that although often subjected to variations, could be employed as a blueprint in the reading and analysis of horror films. This template, which he denominates the 'complex discovery plot', is usually composed of an *onset*, a *discovery*, a *confirmation*, and a *confrontation* stage. As anticipated by Roy Ashbury in his brief study of Murnau's film, these phases and their inevitable diversions from the basic model could be superimposed on *Nosferatu* and used to conduct an in-depth reading of the film's narrative developments.[37]

THE ONSET PHASE

In the onset phase the audience is made aware for the first time of the monster's presence. In Noel Carroll's words:

> We know a monster is abroad and about. The onset of the monster begins the horror tale proper, though, of course, the onset of the monster may be preceded in the narrative by some establishing scenes that introduce us to the human characters and their locales […][38]

The beginning of the film is heralded by a series of three intertitles establishing the time and the place of the action:

> Chronicle of the Great Death in Wisborg. Anno Domini 1838 by

> Nosferatu

> Does this word not sound to you like the midnight call of the Deathbird. Take care in saying it, lest life's images fade into shadows, and ghostly dreams rise from your heart and nourish themselves on your blood.

> Long have I contemplated the origin and recession of the Great Death in my hometown of Wisborg. Here is its story: There lived in Wisborg Hutter and his young wife Ellen.

These three intertitles are just the first example of the wealth of documents, such as diary entries, letters, newspaper clippings etc. that replicate in Murnau's film the multiple-voice narrative employed by Bram Stoker in his novel. The story, a 'chronicle', is immediately identified as the account of real events. We do not know who the unnamed narrator of the story is (although in some French prints of the film – and with a radical diversion from the original script – he is identified as Johann Cavallius/Carvallius, historian of the city of Bremen). What we do know though is that he has received a first-hand account of the events by Hutter himself, as he declares in a subsequent intertitle that we shall discuss later. The three intertitles are also notable because their layout immediately highlights, even on a purely visual level, the key elements in the story. Wisborg, the shadow of death symbolised by the three ominous crosses used as signature, the Great Plague, *Nosferatu* and its link with night and blood, Hutter and Ellen are all mentioned in the space of the film's first few minutes. The onset could hardly be much clearer than this: the spectators are immediately plunged into a story populated by 'shadows and ghostly dreams'.

The first image of the film is an establishing shot that Murnau filmed from the 80m tower of the now destroyed Marienkirche (St Mary's Church) in Wismar. This panoramic shot presents to the viewer a quiet, orderly town with a few people moving about, but the sense of peace is only a fleeting impression for, through the intertitles, we have already been alerted that this situation is destined to change soon and in a dramatic way. The establishing shot is concluded by an iris in and out that introduces us to a scene of marital life between Hutter and Ellen. The first image of Hutter is a medium close-up with the character's back to the camera; his face is reflected in a tiny mirror that barely contains his features, while he is adjusting his tie. Through this shot Murnau immediately plants a couple of subtle but unmistakable hints to Hutter's personality into the spectator's mind: vanity and a lack of perspective seem to be two of its defining traits. Hutter smiles at his reflection and then turns, still grinning, towards the left of the frame. With a quick movement, another clue to his lively but ultimately puerile personality, he turns to the right of the frame and approaches the window in the background of the shot. We now see Ellen surrounded by flowers and playing with a kitten. The mise-en-scène of this short sequence presents her character as someone consistently different from her husband: she quite clearly entertains a strong connection with nature and the contrast between Hutter's cramped mirror and Ellen's window suggests that she is not afraid of looking beyond her immediate horizon. The follow-up of the sequence will give us a further idea about the characters' personalities and the level of interaction and intimacy between them. We cut back to Hutter who runs out of the room towards the right of the screen. Through another iris in and out, Murnau cuts to the garden where Hutter is collecting flowers to make a posy for his wife. While Ellen is busy embroidering, we notice Hutter peaking through the door to observe her. A quick intercut shows us the two characters facing each other, their demeanour completely different: Ellen seems happy but somewhat restrained while facing her husband from across the room, whilst Hutter has the attitude of a mischievous child as he approaches her – 'he laughs and laughs' scribbled Murnau on his copy of the script – hiding the flowers behind his back. When he finally presents her with the posy, Ellen's reaction challenges our expectations: instead of showing appreciation for her husband's romantic gesture, she nurses the flowers with a saddened expression. The intertitle – 'Warum hast Du sie getötet…die schönen Blumen…?!' ('Why did you kill them…the lovely flowers…?!') – not only reiterates her deep tie with nature but also offers to the viewer a new interpretative glimpse into her personality that appears to be melancholic and finely in tune with the idea of mortality. Also the choice of words in the intertitle, 'kill' instead of the more obvious 'pick', seems to reinforce this interpretation: whilst Ellen contemplates nature, Hutter is ready to destroy it and the whole exchange can be read as a premonition of the violence against nature and human, living things that will be brought on by the vampire's arrival in Wisborg. The image following the intertitle is a medium shot of Hutter hugging Ellen to console her, although it is clear from his bemused and condescending expression that he does not really understand his wife's distress, and their body language, just like in the previous short sequence where they embrace and kiss, suggests fraternal affection rather than erotic intimacy. Overall, we leave this sequence behind with a sense of saccharine formality and falseness.

In the following long shot, we see Hutter walking towards the camera on his way to work. A chance encounter with Professor Bulwer offers to the viewer another hint of the danger awaiting him. Out of the blue and for no apparent reason, the Professor warns Hutter that '[…] no one can escape his destiny' and there is no need to be so hasty. This short interlude works as an introduction to the following section of the onset phase where the extent of the danger lurking over Hutter starts taking a darker and more concrete shape. The sequence is introduced by a new intertitle:

> There was also an estate agent called Knock, about whom there were all manner of rumours. One thing was certain: he paid his people well.

Knock's office is presented to the viewer with a series of typical Expressionist traits: it looks cramped, occupied by shelves and littered with piles of papers and documents. The lines of the walls are slanted thus suggesting a sense of oppression and danger. Knock himself is a bizarrely grotesque figure: dressed in an ill-fitting suit, with dishevelled hair and an unhinged look in his eyes, he is perched on a high stool like a monkey on the branch of a tree.

He is unmistakably human but there is also something disturbingly untamed and deranged about his appearance and demeanour that reinforces the connection between him and the feral nature of the Nosferatu himself. In the film's original typescript Knock is thus described:

> Knock's spindly hunch-backed figure. Grey hair, weather-beaten face full of wrinkles. Around his mouth throbs the ugly tic of the epileptic. In his eyes burns a sombre fire.[39]

Another clue to the relationship between Orlok and Knock is represented by the letter covered in a series of mysterious and arcane symbols that we see him reading in a slightly prolonged medium shot. As already mentioned, the strange language used in the letter was put together for the film by Albin Grau and it is the result of the film producer's keen interest in the occult sciences. In volume number 228 of the French magazine *Positif* (1980), Sylvain Exertier conducted an intriguing breakdown of the letter and – although the document has not been entirely deciphered yet – he recognised and explained an ample selection of the symbols and drawings used in the message. The letter should be read from left to right and is marked by what Exertier called a 'relative legibility', a rather striking fact considering that esoteric texts are normally written following the model of *grimoires* – books of spells and magic – that would not be readable without the help of a key that is usually only owned by the ritual's master and his disciples. The symbol opening the letter – a Kabbalistic square enclosed in a circle representing chaos – should function as a key providing the details for the performing of the ritual. The first line of the letter, instead, can be read as a sort of title and it is enclosed in between two Maltese crosses, the symbol of the crusading order of the Knights Hospitalier, that seem to suggest that Count Orlok is indeed about to embark on his own personal crusade. There are many other fascinating symbols used in the letter, such as traditional swastikas representing perseverance and a dragon's head placed before a wavy line suggesting how death will bring destruction coming from across the sea. Exertier and other scholars with him are not conclusive on whether the letter represents a tongue-in-cheek touch in the film or an actual message to fellow occultists: some details, such as the rapidity of the sequences in which the letter is featured and the employment of rather obvious drawings – a dragon, a skull, a snake – to represent common concepts like death and destruction, seem to point in the first direction. At the same time, however, Albin Grau's serious and lifelong involvement with occultism and the interest for the mystical sciences that was widespread amongst many German Expressionist filmmakers would appear to be an indication that what we have here is something deeper and much more complex than a simple cinematographic prop.

Knock's attentive expression and manic laughter contribute to that sense of increasing menace and tension that culminates with the brief dialogue between Knock and Hutter during which the estate agent asks his employee to take care of Count Orlok's desire to buy a house in Wisborg, a job that may cost Hutter: '[…] some effort…a little sweat and…perhaps…a little blood'. After suggesting the young man to offer Orlok the deserted house in front of Hutter's own place, Knock dismisses him with the recommendation to travel quickly to the 'land of ghosts'.

The onset stage proceeds to a short sequence concentrating on Hutter's preparation for his journey to Transylvania. Once again, we have the chance to observe up close the interaction between him and Ellen and to gain further insight into their respective personalities. Hutter's childish enthusiasm about his imminent journey to 'the land of robbers and ghosts' is met by Ellen with a mixture of sadness and foreboding that goes completely unnoticed by her husband. A revealing example of Murnau's use of space composition to build up and comment on the characters' personalities and relations is the layered shot of Ellen standing on the left of the frame while Hutter, separated from her by the partition wall, is running back and forth in the background of the image while he is intent to pack his bags. Ellen's more meditative nature is put here into sharp contrast with Hutter's superficial eagerness. She appears almost to be physically (and, I would add, also emotionally and psychologically) entrapped in the corner of their heavily Biedermeier-style furnished living room, the open window on her right once again subtly hinting at the possibility of an escape into a different reality. The long shawl draped around her shoulders and her posture increase the sense of claustrophobia enveloping her and the wall between Ellen and Hutter acts as a physical metaphor hinting at a much deeper sort of incommunicability. This short sequence also works circularly by anticipating some of the most important elements of the film's closing sequence such as the bed where Ellen will die and the gabled houses across the canal from which the vampire will bring disease and devastation to Wisborg.

Figure 2 Ellen's anguish versus Hutter's childlike enthusiasm

Also the second segment of the sequence reinforces our impression of a relationship based on routine gestures of affection and on a sentimentality shaped by bourgeois conventions: Hutter almost shakes off Ellen's concerned embrace turning away from her and the passionate look he gives to his wife shortly afterwards seems to have little credibility when we compare it with the brief and asexual kiss that follows it. After consigning Ellen, who is by now clad in ominously black attire, in the care of a friend and his sister, Hutter finally leaves Wisborg.

A majestic panoramic night shot of the mountains and forests of the Carpathians marks Hutter's arrival in Transylvania. This shot is particularly important because it can be used to underline a series of major points about Murnau's approach to cinematography. First of all the director's predilection for location shooting marks his distance from Expressionism's obsession on the employment of sets reconstructed in studios. Through the eyes of Murnau natural and urban locations and landscapes go through a poetic treatment and take on deep spiritual – and immensely frightening – resonances that in Expressionist cinema are normally conveyed through the carefully built-up sets. Furthermore, this panoramic view with its strong painterly feeling creates a bridge between Murnau's work and the Romantic tradition of landscape painting where the panorama is transformed into a mental projection shared by the artist and the onlooker who is invited to immerse himself into the meditative qualities of the landscape that can either be uninhabited or occupied by an isolated *Rückenfigur*. As we will see in the book's section devoted to the film's major themes and techniques, the link between painting and cinema was one of Murnau's central concerns and it was also an aspect particularly cherished by the Weimar film industry in its attempt to gain and reinforce an aura of cultural prestige.

The rest of the arrival sequence follows what we can now consider the conventional deployment of the onset phase. Hutter checks into a local tavern to eat and spend the night and urges the innkeeper to feed him quickly for he has to move on and reach Count Orlok's castle. At the very mention of the name, the peasants shudder and recoil in horror and Murnau hesitates on their terrified faces while the landlord warns Hutter of a 'werewolf' lurking in the woods. This short sequence is followed by another nocturnal shot of the nature surrounding the inn. In particular, it is interesting to notice the presence of a rather out of context hyena terrifying a pack of wild horses in a nearby field. Kevin Jackson in his recent book on *Nosferatu* contends that 'these shots […] point to one of the extra-narrative properties which gives the film its richness. *Nosferatu* is, among other things, a cinematic bestiary'.[40] I would also add that the presence of such an incongruous animal such as the hyena – explicitly wanted by Murnau who added a note to this regard in his copy of the script[41] – enhances that sense of estrangement and mystery that is so essential in the overall development of the film's narrative.[42]

From the wide-open space of the outdoor scenes we move into the room where Hutter is about to spend his first Transylvanian night. The room is described as a 'tiny white-washed room with sharp angles: a flickering light from the […] candle'. It is furnished simply but the bed and the arch motive on the back wall, two elements that will become very important in the castle sequences, are placed in a prominent position and occupy an entire half of the shot. After a rapid sequence during which we see Hutter looking outside his window into the night followed by two more shots of the horses and the hyena and of the old peasant women panicking at the sounds coming in from the forest, the onset phase adds a crucial element to our expectations as to what might happen next in the story. By his bedside, Hutter finds a book on 'vampires, monstrous ghosts, sorcery, and the seven deadly sins' and starts reading a page describing a creature of the night known as the *Nosferatu*:

> From the seed of Belial came forth the vampire *Nosferatu* which liveth and feedeth on the Blood of Mankind and, unredeemed, maketh his abode in the frightful caves, graves and coffins filled with accursed Earth from the fields of the Black Death.

In a medium shot we see Hutter reacting to his discovery of the book. The script reads, in Murnau's handwriting: 'Hutter, *shaking his head*, continues reading'; then back to Galeen's original: 'Hutter shuts the book, *having lost interest*. It seems confused to him. He *yawns* and puts out the candle.' His response to the ominous content of the volume is a mixture of amusement and boredom, an attitude that is perfectly in tune with the kind of dismissive and overall shallow personality we have witnessed so far in the film. What we have in this sequence is also a very good example of what Noel Carroll's defines 'phasing':

> […] the audience may put together what is going on in advance of the characters in the story; the identification of the monsters by the characters is phased in after the prior realizations of the audience. That the audience possesses this knowledge, of course, quickens its anticipation […] the audience often is placed in this position

because it, like the narrator, frequently has access to many more scenes and incidents, as well as their implications, than are available to individual characters.[43]

We fade out to black onto the next sequence that carries us smoothly to Hutter's morning departure from the inn during which he has the time to dismiss yet again the *Book of Vampire* and its warnings. Then, through the winding roads in the Carpathians' forests, we find ourselves up the mountain pass where the coach drivers refuse to travel any further thus abandoning their passenger to his destiny. Finding himself alone, Hutter proceeds to cross a bridge that finally marks his entrance to the land of ghosts inhabited by the Nosferatu. The crossing of a material threshold is a crucial *topos* in vampire tales and folklore that tend to proceed along that fine and unstable line separating what is real from what is imaginary, what is normal from what is monstrous. Hutter's passage of the fatal threshold is marked by one of the most famous intertitles in the film:

No sooner had Hutter stepped across the bridge that the eerie visions he had often told me about seized hold of him.

The French Surrealists – starting with André Breton who wrote about *Nosferatu* in his books *Le Surréalisme et la peinture* (*Surrealism and Painting*, 1926) and *Les vases communicants* (*The Communicating Vessels*, 1932) – cherished this narrative passage with particular fondness. What they had in mind, however, was a loosely-translated and incomplete version of the original German ('Kaum hatte Hutter die Brücke überschritten, da ergriffen ihn die unheimlichen Gesichte, von denen er mir oft erzählt hat') that in its French translation reads as 'Et quand il fut de l'autre côte du pont, les fantômes vinrent à sa rencontre' ['And when he crossed the bridge, the phantoms came to meet him']. The French version of the title is certainly more evocative and perhaps even more in line with the nightmarish quality that pervades Murnau's film. However, I find the differences between the two translations to be rather intriguing. The German original stresses yet again the nature of the story as a reported account – later made by Hutter to the anonymous narrator of the story – of the events; his subjective interpretation and subsequent recounting of his adventures are still central. Nevertheless, the intertitle seems to be a bit coy in establishing in an unequivocal manner the supernatural nature of the facts that are being narrated. The very use of the adjective 'unheimlich' which basically means 'un-homely' and therefore can be translated as 'unfamiliar' and 'weird' – and by extension 'uncanny' – retains the implication that there is still a certain degree of hesitation and ambiguity at this stage in the film when it comes to the interpretation of the events we are witnessing. From this point of view, the French translation, which simply cuts off the last part of the German intertitle, is much more forthright and full of a disquieting poetic intensity: 'the phantoms came to meet him': the sights that seize Hutter are not just 'strange' or 'uncanny' but they are active players in the drama unfolding before our very eyes: they are not simple visions but active supernatural presences. The eeriness of the situation is strongly contrasted by the banality of the shot itself: the bridge is nothing more than a tiny footbridge bathed in a strong yellow tint suggesting a bright daylight. Hutter crosses it with no hesitation and for a fleeting moment he turns towards his left to face the camera – and also us, as the audience – with what appears to be a smiling, almost triumphant, expression.

It does not matter though, how much the set up of the shot or the intertitle attempt to convey a sense of harmlessness or of hesitation as to what is about to happen. We know only too well that, once crossed the footbridge with Hutter, we will have entered into the realm of ghosts and the fact that 'things 'look' the same on both sides of the bridge – whether one side represents the 'normal' world while the other harbour phantoms [...]'[44] – makes the situation even more terrifying.

A sinister night shot of Orlok's castle precedes a quick sequence in which we see a coach moving in fast motion along the mountain road. This scene is crosscut with another one showing Hutter proceeding on foot towards the meeting point with his mysterious host. A long shot of a 'snakelike bend' presents Hutter as a diminutive *Rückenfigur* in the bottom-right corner of the screen. For a few seconds, we observe him as he looks towards the dense forest through which the carriage will soon come, approaching from the top part of the screen. A medium shot of Hutter's face alerts us of his astonishment in seeing the odd creature driving the carriage. Henrik Galeen's thus describes the coach and its driver in the film's script:

> [...] A black carriage. [...] Two black horses – griffins? Their legs are invisible, covered by a black funeral cloth. Their eyes like pointed stars. Puffs of steam from their open mouths, revealing white teeth. The coachman is wrapped up in black cloth. His face pale as death. His eyes are staring at Hutter.[45]

With a commanding gesture, the driver invites the now hesitant Hutter to climb inside the carriage that with a narrow U-turn quickly gets back on its way. A close-up shot on a distressed Hutter introduces the viewer to one of the most famous sequences in the film during which, in Murnau's words, the 'Coach drives at top speed through a *white forest!*'.[46]

Figure 3 The ghostly coach riding to Orlok's castle

It is interesting to see how Murnau exploits here cinematic technology – and thus by extension modernity, rationality and progress – to finally introduce the supernatural element into his film. The distortion of reality needed to cause fear and dread in the spectator is achieved not by a pre-styled and reconstructed landscape placed before the camera in the style of Robert Wiene's *Das Cabinet des Dr. Caligari* (*The Cabinet of Dr Caligari*, 1920) but by the way Murnau photographs and edits his natural locations. The washing out of colour turns the natural world into a spectral double whose features seem to resonate with the words used by Maxim Gorky in an article written in July 1896 a few days after his first encounter with the Lumière brothers' cinematograph:

Last night I was in the Kingdom of Shadows. [...] It is a world without sound, without colour. Every thing there – the earth, the trees, the people, the water and the air – is dipped in monotonous grey. [...] It is not life but its shadow, it is not motion but its soundless spectre. [...] Carriages coming from somewhere in the perspective of the picture are moving straight at you [...] And all this in strange silence where no rumble of the wheels is heard [...] Nothing. [...] It is terrifying to see [...].[47]

The use of fast motion to convey fear was obtained simply by the under-cranking of the camera. Rather interestingly, though, this technique did not find many imitators in following films because it became rapidly associated with slapstick comedies that employed acceleration exactly for the opposite reason: to attain humorous effects. In his audio commentary to the BFI edition of the film, Christopher Frayling underlines how 'Murnau's aesthetic here is exactly the opposite of the cinema of the last few decades, which (broadly speaking) uses fast motion for comic effect and slow motion to intensify dramatic impact'.[48] It is also interesting to notice how the entire 'carriage sequence' and more specifically the use of fast motion to signal the arrival of the Nosferatu in the film presents a series of subtle and intriguing elements that resonate with the equivalent passage in the first chapter of Bram Stoker's novel when Jonathan Harker is travelling by coach to the Borgo Pass where he is supposed to meet his host. The coach soon arrives at the Pass but there is no carriage waiting to ferry Harker to his final destination. Just as the driver offers to bring him back to the pass the next day, however,

[...] amongst a chorus of screams from the peasants and a universal crossing of themselves, a caliche, with four horses, drove up behind us, overtook us, and drew up beside the coach. I could see [...] that the horses were coal-black and splendid animals. They were driven by a tall man, with a long brown beard and a great black hat, which seemed to hide his face from us. I could only see the gleam of a pair of very bright eyes, which seemed red in the lamplight, as he turned to us. [...] As he spoke he smiled, and the lamplight fell on a hard-looking mouth, with very red lips and sharp-looking teeth, as white as ivory. One of my companions whispered to another the line from Burger's 'Lenore': - 'Denn die Todten reiten schnell' – ('For the dead travel fast.') The strange driver evidently heard the words, for he looked up with a gleaming smile.[49]

The line quoted in the passage is rightly attributed to Gottfried August Bürger's poem *Lenore*, a dark tale of love and death first published in 1773 that is often considered one of the first examples of 'vampire poems'. The work, although often derided and parodied, remained very popular in Germany well after its first appearance and it would be pretty safe to assume that Murnau was familiar with it and that it would be possible to identify a subtle allusion to the poem – whose line, rather interestingly, should actually be translated with 'for the dead *ride* fast' – in this iconic sequence from the film.

In the following scene a sustained iris shot accompanies us to Nosferatu's castle. The mysterious driver of the demonic carriage with another commanding gesture propels Hutter towards the entrance and we get to see the castle for the first time in a close-up shot: it appears like a solid white façade with a pointy black roof and a solitary small window slightly off-centred. Hutter is thus faced by another – even more momentous – threshold to cross and stands for a handful of seconds in front of the massive wooden door that slowly opens of its own accord allowing him to enter the castle's grounds. A subtle arch motive – that reprises the design of Hutter's bedroom at the inn and that will soon be replicated a number of times within and without the castle – surmounts the building's entrance. Just like in the preceding sequence at the edge of the ghostly forest, Murnau frames his character in a low angle shot presenting him to us as a powerless *Rückenfigur*, dwarfed this time not by nature but by the architectural weight of Nosferatu's fortress and by implication by the destiny that awaits him there.

A reverse shot takes us inside the castle's courtyard that appears to be a rather enclosed space limited by two overlapping arches. Our sense of perspective is further stifled by the pitch-black darkness that we perceive at the furthest end of the shot. It is from this bleak, dark hole that the Nosferatu appears as himself for the very first time: he is a lanky, black-clad figure walking stiffly in our direction, his pointy silhouette strangely replicating the symbol carved in the top part of the screen. When he stops in the middle of the scene the straight-on angle shot lingers on him long enough to make us feel observed and disquieted by his inquisitive and unrelenting eyes that from a distance look like two tiny black holes – even though we know on a rational level that he is waiting for Hutter to arrive, we cannot help but sense a mixture of attraction and repulsion towards that figure that appears to be looking directly at us.

Figure 4 Count Orlok carefully framed inside a series of arches

A cut and another reverse shot take us back to Hutter who is still coming through the castle's gate – yet another arch motive dominates the scene. As we observe him looking around while moving towards the camera, from the privileged position of the high angle shot, we can also see the gate closing behind his back and Hutter jumping at the noise of the slamming doors. It is interesting to notice how the entire sequence, although shot outdoors, is characterised by a powerful sense of claustrophobia. Murnau encloses the space at his disposal within the tight confinement of the arches and through the use of very limited perspective and depth of field. There is always some physical obstruction – the darkness, a wall, the castle's gate behind Hutter's back – that prevents our eyes from wandering further away from the immediate horizon: as soon as he steps into Nosferatu's abode, Hutter – and us along with him – get entangled in his spinning web. When Hutter finally meets Orlok, the two characters are framed in a medium close-up that emphasises both the Count's physical grotesqueness – his long nose, his bushy overdeveloped eyebrows – a real masterpiece of cinematographic make-up envisaged by Albin Grau – and his overpowering presence and authority over his guest who gets told off for having kept the Count waiting 'almost' (as specified by Murnau in the film's script) until midnight. With Orlok preceding Hutter by a few steps, they move towards the arch from where the Count has previously appeared and get swallowed up by its darkness thus completing the film's first act.

The second act in the film opens on an interior shot of the castle's dining room. Galeen describes it as having 'Gigantic dimensions. In the centre a massive Renaissance table. Somewhere in the distance a fire place.'[50] While Hutter is eating, Orlok reads with great attention the mysterious letter previously seen in the hands of Knock.

> The back page of the letter shows a confusion of numbers, legible and illegible letters. The holy number seven is repeated several times. In between, cabbalistic signs. The spindly fingers holding the letter cover up the rest like claws.[51]

Hutter seems mesmerised, 'spell-bound' according to the script, by the sight of his host and, scared by the skeleton clock striking midnight; he cuts his finger while absentmindedly slicing some bread. This is an iconic and often reprised scene that appears in numerous *Dracula*'s adaptations: for the first time, excited by the sight of the 'precious blood' flowing from Hutter's finger, Nosferatu appears to us in all his feral nature. He gets up from his chair and starts moving towards his guest in a threatening way and grabbing Hutter's hand, he attempts to lick the blood away. What ensues is a pseudo-assault during which Hutter pressed on by Orlok is forced to retreat all the way to the fireplace at the back of the dining room. There, going against our expectations, Orlok suggests to an astonished Hutter to spend some time together talking because during the day he sleeps 'the deepest of sleeps'. Duly executing another of Orlok's commanding gestures, Hutter sinks back on the chair behind him: he is nothing but a marionette in the hands of the Count.

The following sequence opens on an intertitle heralding the arrival of the new day that seems to suggest between the lines that Hutter may have been the victim of some sort of nightmare:

> Just as the sun rose, the shadows of the night withdrew from Hutter as well.

An iris out presents us with Hutter still slumped on the chair where we saw him falling the previous night. The mise-en-scène and the character's body posture almost appear as a mirror image of the famous Pre-Raphaelite painting by Henry Wallis *The Death of Thomas Chatterton* (1856) that depicts the tragic passing away of the young Romantic poet.

However, Hutter is not dead and stretching his limbs after a disturbed night of sleep, he starts looking around himself being clearly pleased to see the dining room filled with the bright light of the new day. The following sequence reiterates one of the principles of the onset phase in horror films. Hutter seems to sway between the reassurance provided by the now normal-looking surroundings and the suspect of having been the victim of some mysterious attack. He discovers two tiny punctures on his neck and once again we see a close-up of his face in a small mirror in a scene reprising the opening sequence of the film. And yet, his suspicions are still easily discarded – 'He yawns once more', underlines Galeen in his script.[52] The luscious food prepared on the table is enough to dispel the bad dreams left over by the night and the castle's grounds, surrounded by beautiful forests, seem to be genuinely enjoyed by Hutter who finds himself a cosy spot to write a letter to Ellen. We are still in the phasing stage of the film: our knowledge of what is going on is still a few steps ahead compared to Hutter's. A clear example of this staggered release of information can be found in the letter sequence when Hutter mistakenly connects the punctures on his neck with the harmless mosquitoes that seem to plague the place and his general sense of bewilderment to the 'heavy dreams' caused by the castle's desolation.

A night shot of the forests surrounding the castle – 'another Friedrich moment'[53] – introduces the audience to what can be considered the final section of the onset phase during which events, until now so slowly and carefully presented, will finally take a precipitous turn. The introductory intertitle speaks of the coming of the 'spectral evening light [that] seemed to revive the shadows of the castle' and we return again to the dining room where Hutter and the Count are busy perusing documents and papers. The accidental dropping on the table of a locket containing Ellen's portrait attracts Orlok's attention. He looks at it with wild manic eyes and remarks on the woman's beautiful neck before signing the contract that finalises his acquisition of the deserted house opposite Hutter's. This brief sequence marks Hutter's first glimpse of awareness of what is about to come: Orlok is not simply an isolated eccentric loner but a far more menacing creature whose direct link to the Devil is clearly established in the script: '[…] a satanic look has come into his eyes. His hands have turned into claws'.[54]

A cut takes us to Hutter's bedroom. He kisses softly Ellen's picture and, putting it back into his bag, he is surprised to find in it the book on vampires already seen at the inn. Taking up from the previously read pages, the following two intertitles provide Hutter with further clues about what really goes on at the castle:

> At night this same Nosferatu doth clutch his victim and doth suck like hellish life-potion its blood.

> Take heede that his shadow not encumber thee like an incubus with gruesome dreams.

Made suspicious by the words in the book, Hutter runs to his bedroom's door to look into the dining room: a long shot that goes deep into the dining hall and is immediately followed in dissolve – the only one used in the film – by a medium close-up offers to us the terrifying vision of Orlok as 'a gigantic vampire, a motionless, sombre watcher in the night'.[55] He is standing in front of the fireplace and looks in Hutter's direction bare-headed, with a fixed gaze and its sharp teeth laid bare. Terrified by the vision, Hutter shuts the door, that has neither locks nor handle, and looks for a way out. The shadows engulfing the bedroom transmit an acute sense of claustrophobia and the room's only window opens up on a steep cliff. Hutter, suddenly reverting to a scared child, scrambles towards the bed in search of safety and he is just in time to see the vampire appearing in the doorframe before literally hiding under the covers. In this shot, Orlok's body appears to be perfectly framed within the door's arch and, with the door wide open on the left side of the screen, the overall impression given by the image is that of a propped-up coffin which has suddenly sprung open uncovering the corpse inside it.

At this exact point, the linearity of the events taking place in the castle is interrupted and, through a quick informative intertitle, the action is moved to Ellen's bedroom in Harding's house in Wisborg. The sequence that follows demonstrates a masterful use of cross-cutting. The action, although very cohesive from a chronologically and covering only a handful of minutes, is split spatially between Wisborg and the castle in the Carpathians and its narrative focus alternates between Ellen and Orlok.

Figure 5 Orlok framed in the coffin-like door of Hutter's room

At the beginning of the cross-cut section, we see Ellen getting up from her bed and, attracted by a mysterious force, leaving her bedroom to sleepwalk on the ledge of Harding's balcony. In a secondary cut of the same segment, she is rescued by Harding who also orders to summon a doctor. Back at the castle, Orlok is now attacking Hutter. On the screen we see the shadow of the vampire's claws slowly creeping up on his victim in an image that anticipates the film's closing sequence. We revert back to Ellen, now in bed and surrounded by Harding, his sister and the doctor. She wakes up, sits on the bed and looks off-screen left with a frantic look on her face and starts shouting her husband's name. Back again to the castle: Nosferatu's shadow is moving down towards Hutter who is lying on the bed where he appears to be motionless and unconscious. Unexpectedly, though, the vampire stops and turns around in a left to right direction and with another rapid cut we are transported back to Ellen who in seen in the same pleading position as before. Has the Nosferatu 'heard' the woman's desperate call? The script reads:

Nosferatu turns his head. He is listening intently as if he could feel – hear the [in Murnau's handwriting] terrified shouting in the distance.[56]

The following shift shows him slowly leaving Hutter's room and the entire sequence is closed by the image of an exhausted Ellen who is slowly recovering from what the doctor dismisses as 'harmless congestions of the blood'. This layered sequence is immediately notable for its technical achievements and for the powerful way in which Murnau exploits cinematographic cross-cutting. It is also very important, however, because of its narrative implications: on the one hand, it triggers that frantic and desperate rhythm that will characterise the second part of the film, which will be often constructed along parallel narratives and events revolving around different characters in the story; on the other hand, it also establishes the fundamental psychic link between Ellen and Orlok – who appears to be looking at each other in the sequence's last few segments – that will be at the basis of the film's subsequent events

Figure 6 Cross-cutting: Orlok is distracted from his victim by a mysterious force

The link between Ellen and the Nosferatu is also established clearly by the following intertitle, another extract from the narrator's chronicle:

The doctor related Ellen's distress to me as an unknown illness. I know, however, that her soul that night caught the cry of the Deathbird - Nosferatu was already spreading his wings.

Figure 7 Ellen appearing to plead mercy to the vampire

The link between Ellen and the Nosferatu is also established clearly by the following intertitle, another extract from the narrator's chronicle:

The doctor related Ellen's distress to me as an unknown illness. I know, however, that her soul that night caught the cry of the Deathbird - Nosferatu was already spreading his wings.

THE DISCOVERY PHASE

Proceeding in his analysis of the 'complex discovery plot', Noel Carroll describes the discovery phase as the moment when

> The onset of the creature, attended by mayhem or other disturbing effects, raises the question of whether the human characters in the story will be able to uncover the source, the identity and the nature of these untoward and perplexing happenings.[57]

It is important here to clarify how the discovery phase properly occurs only when it is established beyond any doubt that there is a monster or some supernatural occurrence at the bottom of the problem. In the case of *Nosferatu*, the moment of the discovery can be neatly isolated against the rather extended onset phase during which all the disquieting events directly or indirectly connected to the presence of the vampire had time to pile up before Hutter had any idea of what may be going on.

The quick investigative phase during which Hutter sets out to discover more about the 'horror of his nights' is bracketed by two hauntingly beautiful outdoors night shots marking the sunrise and sundown of his third day in Nosferatu's castle. Suddenly awaken by the daylight, Hutter jumps out of bed clutching his throat and runs out of his bedroom to investigate the castle. We see him running through the pointed arch of his bedroom's door where we last saw the vampire but this time the door is completely removed from the surrounding environment and appears isolated in the middle of a totally black screen. Once again, the door works as a threshold into the supernatural realm of the vampire: in the preceding sequence Nosferatu was framed in it looking like a corpse in his coffin and in this sequence the unnatural seclusion of the passage strongly suggests that Hutter is not crossing an actual door but rather a portal towards the vampire's nightmarish dimension. The long shot encasing the castle's dining room emphasises the eeriness and isolation of the place.

Attracted by an invisible force, Hutter exits the room and rushes to the castle's basement where he finds an old wooden coffin containing the body of the Count suspended in his un-dead state. Although at first only visible past the sarcophagus' battered lid, the close up on Nosferatu's face, with wide open eyes and sharp fangs showing through the half-open mouth, is nothing short of terrifying.

Hutter backs off in horror but gathering again his courage, pushes away the coffin's lid thus exposing the vampire's full body: his pale face and long spindly fingers are emphatically visible against the darkness of his black coat. Hutter's reaction at this vision of horror is one of pure, unmitigated terror. He recoils and falls on the stone staircase behind him and scrambles up the steps without even being able to stand on his feet. After another iris shot of the forest indicating the approaching of the night, we find Hutter slumped on the pavement of his bedroom with a look of bewilderment and fear depicted on his face – '[…] His body is twisted with fear. His hair is standing on end…'[58]. A noise suddenly shakes him from his stupor and looking out of the window he sees, once again in fast motion, Nosferatu loading some coffins onto a cart that dashes off as soon as the vampire has climbed into the topmost sarcophagus. Understanding immediately that Nosferatu's departure will pose a mortal danger to Ellen, Hutter starts ripping off the sheets of his bed to make a rope that will enable him to run away from the castle. Murnau shots him in a close-up while he attempts to climb down the steep walls and then when he crashes to the ground below where he eventually falls unconscious. The frantic pace of the first part of the discovery phase slows down during this last sequence of the film's second act, a beautiful and deceptively peaceful long shot of a flatboat going down a wide river lined by luscious greenery:

> The river flows majestically through the immense plain.
> The scenery is bathed in sunshine.
> All is peaceful.
> Then a large raft appears round a bend in the river and floats slowly into view. Boatmen with long poles are pushing it with considerable effort. At the stern a high pile of boxes. Black, coffinlike boxes. Stacked into a pyramid. An uncanny sight. [Indefatigably, the boatmen go on punting.] The raft is coming closer and closer – like doom.[59]

This vision of approaching disaster lingers on in the mind of the spectator well into the beginning of the film's third act that, again by means of a masterful use of the cross-cutting technique, follows five different narrative strands that work together as a tightly-knit whole in order to conjure and build up the events that will be at the basis of the final two phases in the film: the confirmation stage – although, as we will see, this will never be fully developed in the course of Nosferatu – and the confrontation phase.

The opening sequence of Act III is reserved to Hutter whom we see recovering in a non-descript hospital room (that the script situates in Budapest) where he is assisted by a nun and a doctor. Waking up suddenly from a feverish sleep, Hutter clutches the nun with an expression of terror on his face while shouting the word 'coffins!' A quick insertion of two intertitles connects this opening segment to the second narrative strand of the act that will focus on the tragic journey of the ship *Empusa* and its crew from Galaz to Wisborg. Although called *Demeter*, as in Stoker's novel, in the original script, the ship that will bring Nosferatu to Wisborg was renamed *Empusa* during the making of the film. As pointed out by Kevin Jackson in his book, it would be safe to assume that the rather obscure reference to the *empusa*, a Greek semi-goddess who feasts on the blood of young men while they are asleep, can be probably regarded as a contribution by Albin Grau to the film's virtual list of intertextual references, along the lines, for instance, of the allusion to Burger's poem *Lenore* in the sequence of the fast moving ghostly white carriage discussed earlier in this chapter.[60] The quayside sequence starts off with a routine check of the ship's cargo – six crates of earth (and not simple sand, as Murnau points out twice in the script) for experimental purposes – that turns out to contain more than just soil: a multitude of rats swarms out of the box that has been opened for controls by the port's authorities. The viewer is here invited to make an immediate – although perhaps still subconscious – connection between the rats and those stories chronicling the spreading out of plague epidemics by means of sea travels. The implication seems clear: it is not just Nosferatu who is coming to Wisborg: he is also carrying the plague in his trails.

In a first apparent non sequitur, the dockyard sequence is linked to the third set of action of this narrative section of the film. Back to Wisborg, Professor Bulwer, the Paracelsian doctor whom we saw briefly with Hutter at the beginning of the film, is giving a lecture on the dark side of nature to a small group of his students. In a rapid sequence made up of four short segments, Murnau puts into connection the various examples of predators (a Venus flytrap, a polyp with its tentacles, and a spider) selected by Bulwer and presented to the audience through clips – beautifully tinted and shot in micro-cinematography – taken from scientific films with the predatory madness of the estate agent Knock (who, in the meantime, has been secluded in an asylum), and more widely with the now-approaching Nosferatu.

While Bulwer describes the Venus flytrap eating a fly by comparing it to a vampire, the film cuts to Knock who, equally, is catching and eating flies in front of the bewildered doctor Sievers. This parallel between the rapacious side of the natural world and the greed for blood ('Blood is life!' exclaims Knock in the sequence) of the vampire and of his slave will be reiterated two more times through the examples of the incorporeal – 'almost but a phantom' – polyp feeding off a microscopic organism and the spider entangling an insect in its web. The connection is particularly intriguing and

Just as Bulwer compares the carnivorous plant to the vampire, Murnau's editing compares the madman and the scientist, each the center of a dark system of deadly metaphors and hysterical imitations.[61]

Although pertaining to the limbo between life and death, Nosferatu, suggests Murnau, is also a manifestation of the dark side of the natural world: he maliciously preys on living things, like the carnivorous Venus flytrap or the spider; just like the polyp he can make himself incorporeal and his natural voyage companions are the rats travelling with him in the boxes full of his native Carpathians' soil.

The following segment acts as a short melancholic interlude that shifts the film's narrative focus from the vampire to Ellen. A quick set of intertitles provide the set-up for what is about to come:

Ellen was often seen on the beach within the solitude of the dunes. Yearning for her beloved, her eyes scanned waves and distance alike.

An iris out presents her to the audience in a medium long shot while she is sitting on a solitary bench along a windy beach dotted with several crosses bent by the relentless wind. The original script – which, slipping back into Stoker's novel, names the place as 'the graveyard of Whitby', a mistake that was subsequently corrected by Murnau to 'Heligoland' – suggests a rather different set up for the scene:

[…] a long row of benches. People are strolling up and down looking out on to the sea…sitting on the benches and enjoying the view.[62]

Compared to the much more mundane initial idea suggested in the script by Galeen, what we have on film is an infinitely more haunting and melancholic representation. Ellen's solitude and concern are heightened by her physical isolation from other human beings and also by her demeanour and attire. She appears on the beach in the attitude of a *Rückenfigur* – thus investing the sea with the extra function of becoming a mirror for her turbulent state of mind – and the beach seems to be completely devoid of other signs of life and is on the contrary full of reminders of death and loss (e.g. the crosses, the black dress). Amongst the crosses, Ellen appears as an authentic 'woman in black' who is more likely to be mourning someone's passing rather than waiting for someone's return. The desolation of the scene is almost immediately contrasted with the cheerful images of Harding and his sister playing croquet (another of Murnau's specific requests apparent from one of his handwritten corrections in the script) in the garden of their villa. Their game is interrupted by an old servant who has just received a letter from the postman. Realising that the letter is indeed from Hutter, Harding and Anny rush to the beach to consign the letter to Ellen in the hope of giving her some relief from her distress.

Figure 8 Ellen longing for her lover

A series of outdoors views of the wavy sea and of the wind-battered sand dunes contribute to increase even further the sense of isolation and solitude conveyed by the location and it is also interesting to notice how differently Murnau presents the two female characters in the sequence. Despite being clearly the same age, Ellen looks old and world-weary when compared to Anny who is described in the script as 'glad' and 'quick' and ready to burst into 'a joyful laugh'. The contrast between them is not simply marked by the black versus white attires the two characters are wearing but it is also conveyed by their body posture and general demeanour. Feeble and burdened by worries, Ellen does not even have the strength to get up when she sees Harding and Anny approaching and, even more importantly, she refuses to open and read Hutter's letter asking instead Anny to do it on her behalf. The following intertitles present to us the letter we saw Hutter writing after his first night at the castle. Images of Anny reading the letter alternate with medium close ups of Ellen listening intently to its contents. At the mention of the 'mosquito bites' troubling Hutter, though, something seems to stir Ellen into action: she grabs the letter from Anny's hands and finishes her reading. Clearly sensing something untoward – and thus confirming the impression of a supernatural psychological link between her and the Nosferatu already hinted at during the sequence of the second assault on Hutter – Ellen gives way to her fears and leaves the scene running away from her bewildered friends.

By means of another jump in location, we are back in Budapest where Hutter is trying to recover from his ordeal, just in time to see him leave the hospital room directed home 'by the shortest route'. Hutter's departure is followed by two quick sequences suggesting the competition between him and Orlok in their rush to get to Wisborg: in the first sequence the Empusa is filmed while it is slowly crossing the screen right to left. Alone in the open sea and apparently devoid of any life (there are no sailors visible on the deck) the ship is a stark reminder of the doom looming over Ellen and the rest of the population in Wisborg. In contrast with the ship's smooth sailing, the next scene shows Hutter leading his horse through a dense and intricate portion of vegetation where his movements appear to be particularly difficult. As if to reiterate and underline the smoothness of the vampire's journey – because quite clearly the dead not only ride but also sail fast – Murnau intercuts another shot of the Empusa crossing again the screen right to left. Nosferatu's advantage over Hutter appears now to be obvious and insurmountable. The film's incessant cross-cutting continues and through an iris out we are back into Knock's solitary cell where we see him steal a newspaper from the back pocket of an asylum attendant. Once alone, Knock 'unfolds the paper [trembling with expectancy] and starts reading [searching for something] with wide-open eyes'.[63] The subsequent intertitle reproduces the newspaper's page chronicling the explosion of a plague epidemic:

PLAGUE. A plague epidemic has broken out in Transylvania and the Black Sea ports of Varna and Galaz. All victims exhibit the same peculiar stigmata on the neck, the origin of which still puzzles the doctors. The Dardanelles were closed to all ships suspected of carrying the plague.

As a side note, it is interesting to notice that the edition of the film released by Eureka has omitted one line from the English translation of this intertitle. Where the original German title reads: 'Junge Leute warden in Massen hingerafft' ('Young people are being swept away in large numbers') the English intertitle jumps straight onto the next line. It is an omission that I tend to attribute to a simple oversight but that it nevertheless detracts from the chronicle another disturbing detail connecting Nosferatu to its young, unsuspecting victims that adds a further note of meaningless tragedy to the whole story. The sequence closes with a triumphant-looking Knock who smiles with 'an expression of demonic grandeur' knowing that the plague is no coincidence but it is the signal marking Orlok's arrival.[64] Another alternation of Hutter's slow journey by land and of the Empusa – now filmed through a series of dramatic close-ups of its sails that enhance the looming character of the ship – anticipates a longer sequence taking place on the ship where we see one of the crewmen alerting the Captain to the fact that one of the sailors has fallen ill and is below deck in a delirious state. After paying a quick visit to the sailor, the Captain and the mate leave him alone to rest in the ship's hold. The change, from amber to blue, in the image's tint suggests the passing of time. It is now night and the sailor turning around towards the boxes that have always been visible lurking in the background of the shot, is terrified by the vision of an incorporeal image of Nosferatu hovering over the coffins. A new cut takes us back again to Hutter who is now seen dragging his horse that appears to be slightly limping on the rugged terrain.

The following intertitle will inform us of the tragic destiny of the crew travelling on the Empusa:

It [the plague] spread through the ship like an epidemic. The first stricken sailor pulled the entire crew after him into the dark grave of the waves. In the light of the sinking sun, the captain and ship's mate bid farewell to the last of their comrades.

Back on the ship's deck and after the sombre burial at sea of the last crewman, the ship's mate grabs an axe and prepares to go below deck. An intense profile close-up communicates his resolve to see into the curse that has befallen on the ship even though his attitude is contrasted by the captain's resigned demeanour. Another quick intercut back to Hutter: he is now riding his horse 'at tremendous speed' left to right across the screen and along a desolate plain. Back on the Empusa and this time below the ship's deck. The mate starts axing away at the coffins only to be met by swarms of rats until we see him freezing in a pose of surprise and terror. In a reverse shot introducing one of the most famous sequences in the film, we see the reason of his reaction: stiff as a corpse, a terrifying Jack-in-the-box, Nosferatu springs up from one of the coffins in 'an image simultaneously suggesting erection, pestilence, and death'.[65]

In a mad panic, the mate rushes back to the deck and throws himself in the water under the astonished eyes of the captain. The destiny of the Empusa is now about to reach full circle and Murnau films it at a relentless pace: we see the captain binding himself with ropes to the wheel – 'Thus he awaits the horror…'[66] – in one last desperate attempt to remain at his place of command until the end of his doomed journey and immediately after Murnau frames Nosferatu walking across the deck in a low angle shot from the ship's hold. The lack of any real depth in the image and the ship's masts framing the black and lanky silhouette of the Count increase the sense of tragedy and domination already conveyed by the situation.

Before finally fading to black, the lingering shot on the terrified captain tells us without showing anything of all the horror of his final demise. The following intertitle – 'The ship of death had acquired its new captain' – along with the long 'contre jour' shot of the Empusa that appears majestic and black against the night sky conclude the film's third act on a note of doom and tragedy that is however not entirely devoid of an underlying sense of awe and poetic beauty that Kevin Jackson interestingly connects to Edmund

Figure 9 Low-angle shot of Orlok taking possession of the Empusa

Burke's definition of the 'Sublime' as '[a] mode of beauty associated with awe, fear and even pain rather than health, pleasure and calm.'[67]

The opening minutes of the film's fourth act employ again the cross-cutting technique to build up the narrative tension for Nosferatu's arrival in Wisborg. Taking its cue from an intertitle underlining the supernatural origin of the ship's movement – 'Nosferatu's deadly breath swelled the sails of the ship, which flew on toward its destination with ghostly haste' – and from a sequence filmed from the ship's prow that could be compared to an eerie version of early phantom ride films (during which a camera mounted on the front of a moving vehicle would take the audience on journeys to exotic locations and foreign countries), the images cut quickly to Ellen who is about to fall prey to another attack of somnambulism and subsequently to the stormy sea – thus underlining once again the connection between her and the vampire – and finally to Hutter who is now seen approaching home travelling on a coach. Awoken by the storm, Anny gets up to look for her friend and finds Ellen in a semi-trance on the villa's terrace.

Figure 10 A contre-jour shot of the ship of death

Her words – 'I must go to him. He's coming!!!' – intercut both with images of the Empusa and of Hutter on his way to Wisborg have often struck the film's commentators as being deeply ambiguous. Who is Ellen really talking about? Who must she meet so urgently? The psychological link between her and Orlok, along with what has been seen by some as a possible erotic infatuation for the repulsive but ultimately animalistic character of the vampire, a figure that traditionally presents strong sexual undertones, complicate and muddle a simple interpretation of Ellen's words. Although it is true that this sense of ambiguity is resolved on a pure narrative level by placing strategically a sequence focusing on Hutter after the intertitle with Ellen's words, this uncertainty cannot be shaken off easily and is subtly reinforced by the fact that Murnau alternates close ups of Orlok's ship with long shots of Hutter's journey, thus giving the impression that Ellen's urgency is in fact due to the incoming schooner and not the arrival of her husband who seems to be – also on a simple visual level – still far away from his final destination. Another cut on the Empusa, filmed this time from a different angle, is followed by Ellen running out of the house in her nightgown and by a sequence focusing on Knock who, guessing the arrival of Orlok, is growing increasingly agitated.

The scene in the mental asylum is followed by another one of the film's iconic sequences: in a long and sustained shot Wisborg's harbour is obliterated by the 'dead and forsaken'[68] ship that slides ominously right to left across the screen virtually cancelling all signs of human life from the town in its path. Knock senses that Orlok has finally arrived in town. Cut back to the Empusa where the ship's hatch gets lifted by a mysterious force: Nosferatu, showing a malicious grin on his face, peaks out of the hatch while Knock manages to escape from the asylum.

Framed in the archway of one of Wisborg's medieval doors, 'Nosferatu, coffin under his arm [is] looking around to orientate himself. Then he strides on'.[69] Swift cut on his rats that are now seen swarming out of the ship. Through another quick parallel montage, Murnau films Hutter's and Orlok's end of the journey: whilst Hutter finally reunites with Ellen, who collapses in his arms on the threshold of their home, Orlok keeps striding through Wisborg. We see him passing through the little square with the fountain that we saw twice at the beginning of the film and then stopping knowingly just outside the house of the unsuspecting couple who are overpowered by the happiness of their reunification. Cut to the empty warehouse opposite Hutter's: Nosferatu is slowly approaching it crossing the canal on a small barge. Using again his background in art history for inspiration, Murnau frames and films the action in such a way that the entire sequence can be read as a clear and unmistakable homage to Arnold Böcklin's painting *Isle of the Dead* (1866). The nocturnal spectral quality of the scene is conveyed visually by the supernatural movement of the little boat that appears to glide across the water by itself while the figure of the vampire stands still in the darkness. Once outside the warehouse, the vampire will simply disappear into it by means of a very effective and eerie image dissolve.

The morning after Nosferatu's arrival in Wisborg the town authorities find themselves facing the riddle of the Empusa. In a rather short but lively sequence, Murnau films Harding and other dignitaries investigating the empty schooner, and collecting the ship's log and the captain's diary to try and unravel its mystery. In the town hall, where the mise-en-scène recalls the famous painting by Rembrandt the *Anatomy Lesson* (1631), the doctor and the other men examine the body of the dead captain and the two tiny punctures visible on his neck. We see Harding reading from the ship's log about rumours of a 'strange passenger' hiding on board and about the presence of rats in the ship's hold. The conclusion seems obvious: the crew has been exterminated by the plague carried by the rats. Panic strikes: the men quickly leave the town hall, some of them covering their mouths with a handkerchief. The closing sequence of the film's fourth act plants a note of quiet desperation in the mind of the viewer. An iris out is followed by a long shot of a steep and deserted street: the radical sense of perspective, which is stretched out to a haunting and almost irrational extreme, and the heavy shadows occupying a prominent portion of the shot convey a sense of stifling narrowness and immobility. The only person about town is the local crier who reads out a proclamation on how to act in order to contain the plague epidemic; Murnau lingers with his camera on the terrified faces of various citizens who start retreating hastily indoors at the mention of the plague.

The film's final act opens up with a short sequence chronicling the macabre business of counting the victims of the plague epidemic. An iris out introduces a medium shot of an old town official checking out a row of houses and marking with a white cross the doors of those places where people have been afflicted by the plague – a group of black-clad pallbearers is filmed while carrying out a coffin from one of the homes. A new intertitle moves the action back to Ellen and Hutter:

> Hutter made Ellen swear not to touch the book which had frightened him with its visions. - Yet she could not resist its bizarre attraction.

In a close-up shot we see Ellen reading the Book of Vampire, her agitation, along with a creeping sense of awareness, increasing after each word. The pages of the book are projected onto the screen and thus we discover that the only way to defeat the vampire is through the sacrifice of 'a maiden wholly without sin [who] maketh the Vampyre forget the first crow of the cock' by giving 'freely of her blood'. At this point Hutter comes into the room and 'with agitation, almost hostility he grabs the book' from Ellen's hands.[70] In his gesture, and in his warning not to even touch the book - we can read another trait of Hutter's typical lack of maturity and perspective, as if ignoring the shadows would be enough to make them go away. Ellen shakes away from his embrace and turns to the window pointing out nervously towards the empty houses that can be seen in the image's background. Desperately and almost impatiently, she shows to her husband what she has been seeing every night through her window: a long shot of the empty warehouses and, almost indistinguishable behind one of the windows on the left of the shot, Nosferatu looking in her direction.

Hutter runs to the window but shakes his head in a desperate act of disbelief; Ellen walks slowly away from the room leaving her husband fall onto the bed in complete desperation. The script underlines here in a very effective manner the gap in knowledge and awareness experienced by the two characters:

> [Ellen] knows all she has to know. Hutter has not come to that yet. He finds her calmness disturbing. He follows the retreating figure with his eyes. [...] Hutter, despairingly, presses his fists against his face.[71]

The whole sequence leaves the viewer with a series of open questions. Why is Hutter so stubborn in denying what it is really going on in Wisborg? Why does he not try instead to unburden himself of his terrible experiences and worst fears by recounting his adventures to those closest to him?

THE CONFIRMATION PHASE

In the ideal template of Noel Carroll's 'complex discovery plot', this would be the perfect time for the confirmation phase, which 'involves the discoverers of or the believers in the existence of the monster convincing some other group of the existence of the creature and of the proportions of the mortal danger at hand [...].[72] In *Nosferatu* the transition into the confirmation stage would appear to be rather smooth, especially considering the fact that Ellen seems to be already strangely abreast of the terrible events that are taking place in Wisborg and of the connection between the mysterious figure looking at her from across the canal and the plague that is decimating the town's inhabitants thus rendering for Hutter virtually unnecessary the act of convincing other people of the existence of the monster that often takes up a large part of the confirmation stage. However, in Murnau's film this phase gets strangely frustrated. At no time during the film Hutter conveys his knowledge of the vampire to Ellen – or to any other character for that matter – although we know that after the events, he does recount his story to the film's narrator. On the contrary, he tries to prevent his wife from reading the *Book of Vampire* and he obstinately refuses to acknowledge her awareness of the existence of the monster. The other characters in the story are equally blind or kept away from the truth. Even the Paracelsian Professor Bulwer who seems, or at least should be, in tune with the mysterious forces lurking in nature's darkest corners fails by the end of the film to make the connection between the plague and *Nosferatu*. Thus his narrative function gets completely drained of any possible centrality: if in Stoker's novel Van Helsing is the real driving force behind the understanding of the events and of the plot that will bring to the final dispatching of the monster, in *Nosferatu* Bulwer turns out to be a rather inane and pathetic figure, incapable of leaving any remarkable trace in the story.

The arrival of another night in the terrified town of Wisborg is marked by Murnau with a beautiful night shot of a street lamp-lighter going about his business in a dark alley. Although seemingly shot outdoors, the mise-en-scène in this brief sequence is marked by a remarkably Expressionist feeling of oppression and entrapment which is mainly conveyed by the sparse lighting and by the encumbering presence of the walls that restrict our field of vision to a very narrow space in the middle of the screen.

Through a dissolve and an intertitle underlining the widespread fear clutching the town, the action is transferred back to Harding's villa where we find him trying to calm down a highly distressed Anny. Harding leaves to fetch the doctor and from the change in the image's tint we know that the action is now taking place at night: a mysterious fluttering of the curtains sends Anny into a panic. We see her frantically trying to summon the servant to her room for help but, failing to do, she collapses onto the floor. The original sequence outlined in the script by Galeen was far heavier handed in its use of supernatural elements:

> Anny, having almost fainted with fear, comes to again. She opens her eyes. She lifts up her head. Nobody around?? Is she all alone?? Isn't there something moving about in the corner? Something fluttering at the window?

> The window, covered by the curtain. Behind it, the shadow of a giant bat.

It grows and grows. Soon it isn't a bat any longer.

A vampire?! NOSFERATU?![73]

However, the suggestive and almost poetic restraint on the supernatural features applied by Murnau to this sequence is truly remarkable and contributes to making it all the more frightening and disquieting.

THE CONFRONTATION PHASE

Cut back to Ellen who is now observing from her window a long procession of coffins that stretches out all the way up the narrow street we have already seen at the beginning of the fourth act. She falls to her armchair in desperation and picks up again the *Book of Vampires* where she reads again the passage about the 'maiden without sin' as the sole means of salvation from the vampire's curse. Her reaction is almost surprising and she faces the camera with a stern air of determination – 'Ellen lifts up her head, staring into space like a visionary. She knows. […]'–[74] before Murnau dissolves the image into the next intertitle.

A group of citizens is seen discussing the acts and whereabouts of Knock. Murnau lingers on their emaciated features and fanatical eyes long enough to convey the sense of doom and fear experienced by the people in Wisborg. Cut on a long shot of a narrow side street: Knock is filmed running towards the camera while a large crowd is chasing him. The sequence is lively paced and full of changes of perspective: a high angle shot of an empty street is followed by a low angle that frames Knock crouching on a roof-top. An iris shot closes in onto his hideous and deranged features that are now more animal-like than ever before in the film. Climbing down the roof, Knock continues his escape running off screen left. Brief cut to Ellen who is embroidering the words 'I love you' onto a cushion. Back to Knock who, passing by the camera, is now seen leaving the town and rushing away towards the open countryside while he is still being chased by the angry mob. A long iris shot frames a black silhouette that will turn out to be a scarecrow that gets immediately attacked by the crowd. Murnau films the whole sequence using the 'contre jour' technique and maintaining a certain distance from the action that thus appears to be even more savage and violent.

A beautiful night shot of the calm sea lit up by the moon is immediately followed by the hideous image of Nosferatu clinging like a spider onto the window frame of the empty warehouse. The half-open mouth shows the sharp fangs and his eyes spark with a look of yearning and lasciviousness. Cut to Ellen asleep in her bed. She wakes up suddenly and turns towards the window in the direction of the warehouse clutching at her chest with an indefinable expression that could be interpreted either as fear or desire to go to the window. A slightly larger shot of the room shows Hutter asleep in an armchair nearby the bed. There is a sense of distance between him and Ellen that is powerfully expressed by the mise-en-scène of the sequence: the demarcation lines drawn up by the bedframe and by the vertical white frame dividing the window in two sections create a physical gap between the two characters that contrasts strongly with the palpable connection that is instead taking place between Ellen and Orlok: a disturbed and disturbing love triangle is being acted out in front of our eyes. Rising slowly from her bed, Ellen walks to the window and is about to open it. Cut to Nosferatu who starts moving imperceptibly and then back to Ellen who hesitates and pulls back from the window. She turns right towards her husband who is placidly and obliviously asleep in the armchair. The expression on Ellen's face is one of desperation and disappointment: she looks at Hutter like a mother frustrated with a naughty child would. This glance marks the turning point in the whole sequence: Ellen finally opens the window thus silently inviting Nosferatu in her home. Although contrasting with previous scenes, such as Anny being attacked in her room, Ellen's invitation to the Count is in line with traditional vampire folklore according to which a vampire cannot enter someone's house unless explicitly invited in. Recent films and TV series, such as Let the Right One In (Tomas Alfredson, 2008) or Buffy the Vampire Slayer (Joss Whedon, 1997-2003) have made effective use of this element and in Bram Stoker's novel, it is up to Van Helsing to clarify this point in his overview of the vampire's strengths and weaknesses in Chapter XVIII:

> He may not enter anywhere at the first, unless there be some one of the household who bid him to come; though afterwards he can come as he please.[75]

Nosferatu is now approaching fast — we see him leaving the warehouse — and Ellen, in a state of frantic agitation, wakes Hutter up and begs him to go fetch Professor Bulwer. A creepy shot of the now truly empty warehouses is followed by the iconic sequence of Nosferatu's shadow creeping up the stairs on his way to Ellen's bedroom.

Figure 11 Shadow play: the iconing image of the vampire approaching his victim

Cut back to Ellen who is waiting for the vampire on her bed. The whole sequence conveys a mixed feeling of fear and yearning that culminates in the shadow of Nosferatu's hand apparently clutching Ellen's heart causing her to quiver. It is interesting to notice how in this scene, as in all the sleepwalking sequences, Ellen is not dressed in her customary black attire but wears instead a white and slightly transparent nightgown: her dress characterises her as the sacrificial victim but also as the virginal bride who can destroy the vampire through her absolute purity, a subtle clue that seems to suggest that she has never consummated her marriage with Hutter but is instead ready and willing for the sake of humanity to do that with Orlok. A quick cut back to Hutter who is now desperately trying to shake Bulwer from his torpor, and then once more Murnau moves the action back to its narrative fulcrum: Ellen's bedroom is bathed in darkness and, barely visible in the left bottom corner of the screen, we can distinguish Nosferatu's white skull. He is reclined over Ellen's supine body and he is busy sucking her blood. The last few minutes of the film are once again characterised by an engaging use of the cross-cutting technique. A brief scene informs us that Knock has been finally apprehended and took back to the mental asylum. This sequence is followed by another shot of Nosferatu sucking Ellen's blood and, more importantly, by an image of a rooster marking the beginning of the new day. The screeching of the bird seems to alert the vampire as to what it is about to happen and we see him slowly raise his head – '[…] drunk with pleasure'[76] – from Ellen's chest. Cut to Knock back in his cell where he is sensing that something terrible is occurring to his 'master'. In an outdoors shot, Hutter and Bulwer are walking back towards Hutter's place. Other cuts: first to Knock and then to the bedroom that is getting slowly filled up with the light of the new day rising. Nosferatu raises up from Ellen's body and walk slowly towards the window: it is clear from his expression that he knows his time is up. In a medium shot Nosferatu clutches his chest in a gesture replicating Ellen's and, touched by the sunlight, he slowly fades away leaving behind a tiny puff of white smoke. The last scene – preceded by Knock confirming the vampire's death – 'The master…is…dead' – focuses at first on Ellen waking up apparently unscathed by her night's ordeal and happily aware of having won the uneven fight against the monster. Almost immediately, however, she collapses back onto her pillow just in time to see Hutter coming back accompanied by Bulwer. Hutter takes Ellen in his arms but the young woman dies soon after. One of the last images in the film is a long indoors shot of Hutter's house: in the background the young man is crumpled on the bed where his wife has just died and in the foreground the pathetic and ineffectual figure of Professor Bulwer is sadly shaking his head at the sight of the tragedy that is taking place behind him. One last intertitle:

> Witness the miracle on the heels of the truth: at that very hour, the Great Death came to an end, and as if confronted by the victorious radiance of the living sun, the shadow of the Deathbird was dispersed.

And one last haunting image: Nosferatu's castle now lying in ruins – '[…] as if Orlok's lair has come tumbling down now that its denizen has finally been laid to rest.'[77]

CHAPTER 4 – SIGNS AND MEANINGS

4.1 *NOSFERATU*'S STYLE AND FORM

Despite having been produced in the early 1920s, *Nosferatu*, especially when watched in its original cut and with its tints and tones restored, is still an incredibly remarkable and powerful film. Murnau's eye for complex and layered mise-en-scène and his rhythmical sense of editing confer to the film a compelling visual quality and a narrative that is both engaging and creepily uncanny.

In order to analyse a film thoroughly, we should always take into account the elements that constitute a film's grammar and syntax: mise-en-scène, camerawork, editing, and sound, although normally discussed separately, must be thought of as interconnected and inter-dependent. The mise-en-scène – that is to say, all that is visible on the screen at any given moment – is constituted by a large number of different elements that can be roughly divided in pre-cinematic features (such as sets, costumes, light, etc.) and cinematographic elements (camera angles, distance, focus and so on).

Sets and locations are amongst a film's most immediate and visible features. In *Nosferatu*, sets and locations are used in a highly creative and innovative way. The film is not characterised by the typical Expressionist sets that, reconstructed in large movie studios, generally hinted at the existence of a partially or wholly imaginary fantastic and delusional world as in the case of Robert Wiene's *Das Cabinet des Dr. Caligari* or Fritz Lang's *Metropolis*. On the contrary, the film employs real locations and realistic interiors that are subsequently invested with a poetic treatment that enhances their atmosphere to the point of transforming them into highly meaningful entities that do not simply act as backdrop for the characters but underline specific psychological or narrative passages without being too obtrusive or heavy-handed, as it happens on occasion in more traditionally realised Expressionist films. The real locations used in *Nosferatu*, amongst them the Carpathians mountains, the wild river along which the vampire's coffins are transported on a barge, the lingering night shots of forests that at times interrupt the action, the roaring sea filmed from the schooner taking Orlok to Wisborg, transmit a profound sense of supernatural events lurking in the shadows of reality – they are chilled by what Béla Balázs called 'the glacial draughts of air from the beyond'[78] – and

[…] for all the increased directness, all the unyielding photographic naturalism of these scenes, something, one senses, remains elusively beyond what the camera can capture. The physical world, placed almost tangibly before our eyes, is still somehow distant, inscrutable, ghostly.[79]

If the outdoors locations straddle the line between fantasy and naturalism, the sets reconstructing the indoor sites – Hutters' home in Wisborg, Knock's office, Orlok's castle and such – tend to present elements that can enrich our understanding of the relationships and power struggles at work in the film. For instance, in the scenes where Ellen and Hutter interact, Murnau often places some obstructive element in-between the two characters, such as a door or a bed frame, to increase the underlying impression of incommunicability that can be repeatedly perceived in their interaction as a couple. The sense of stifling respectability that triggers Ellen's ultimate rebellion/ sacrifice is equally conveyed in the film by the heavy Biedermeier interiors of her marital home. Albin Grau, in his role as the film's set designer, fills up Hutter's home to the brim with flowery wallpaper, tiny portraits, wooden cabinets and furniture that seem to suggest a heaven of peace and conventional sentimentality. At the same time though, this same heaven is pierced through and through by the high number of windows, mirrors, and doors that deconstruct the space and unsettle its neatly organised structure. The décor becomes at once an index of the period and a subtle critique of bourgeois conformism (see figure 2).

Another good example of an apparently simple décor used as a hint to the balance of power amongst the film's characters can be identified in the chequered floor that appears in the sequence of Hutter's first night in Orlok's castle.

The resemblance of the floor to a chess-board, along with the blocking scheme applied by Murnau to his actors on the set, subtly but unmistakably suggests to the spectator that once entered into the castle, Hutter has become a piece in the strategy game played by Orlok in his plan to move from his remote Carpathians abode to the teeming streets of Wisborg. The power of this short sequence thus derives largely from the tension implied in the contrast between the apparently innocent set up – a large but otherwise rather non-descript castle dining hall – and the precise execution of the delicate manoeuvre that Orlok is plotting at the expense of Hutter.

Figure 12 Suggestive use of décor: the chess-board floor in Orlok's castle

The employment of recurrent architectural motifs such as arches, doorways, stairs, and bridges is another striking feature in the mise-en-scène of *Nosferatu*. Murnau frequently frames or limits his shots by means of arches; think for example of the series of arched shapes that provide the visual boundaries to Orlok's first appearance towards the end of the film's first act (see figure 4) or of the doorframe shaped as a pointed arch that encases the vampire in the attack sequence discussed in the close reading section of this book. By framing and enclosing the subjects, the arches also act as a visual reminder of the sense of threat that is closing in around the innocent characters in the film – for instance, when Hutter enters his tiny bedroom in the inn, there is a prominent arch in the background of the image that eerily anticipates the arched door of his room in the castle where he will be attacked by the vampire.

The other architectural elements featured in the film are all connected with the aspect of liminality that is an integral part of vampire mythology and more generally of supernatural stories where often the crossing of a threshold – into a haunted mansion, a forbidden forest or a parallel dimension – provide the connective link between reality and the other world: Hutter crosses two bridges before entering into Orlok's castle, Ellen sleepwalks along the ledge of Harding's terrace in a state of trance, the mate on the Empusa descends the stairs into the schooner's hold to try and unravel the origins of the mysterious illness that is taking over the ship: these are just a few examples of how Murnau manages to exploit transitional spaces by charging up their everyday appearance and function with deeper psychological and narrative implications. Thus, very subtly but in an unmistakable manner, the film finds itself in a web of references that stretch from the in-betweenness of the vampire's body – who is dead and alive at the same time – to the liminal nature of cinema itself where each image exists on the threshold between light and darkness, reality and its reproduction and comes to life only to be exhausted and 'killed' by/into the following frame.

The employment of frames, thresholds and passageways as visual clues is also linked inextricably with the recurrent act of violating and trespassing them. This action does not simply take the story's events forward but could also be interpreted as the visual representation of some of the deeper motives at work in the film that sees in the dynamics between outside and inside one of its main narrative hinges. The first image of the film, moving in from a panoramic shot of Wisborg into Hutter's home, immediately suggests a sense of contrast between the apparently safe heaven of home and the menace that can come from without those familiar boundaries. The whole narrative of *Nosferatu*, and of Stoker's novel before it, appears in effect to be permeated by the foreboding of a threat coming from outside and the vampire has been interpreted at times as the embodiment of the fear of the foreign Eastern European intruder who lands in Germany to violate its women and kill its men thus destroying the inner fabric of German society.

Although often remembered for the daring and innovative camera movements devised for his later films, such as *The Last Laugh* (1924) shot by Karl Freund in 1924, Murnau's choice for the camerawork in *Nosferatu* appears to be of an entirely different nature: in this film the camera does not move much. The only notable movements are a few panoramic shots – for instance, those surveying the majestic Carpathian mountains – and the shots of the schooner sailing to Wisborg that were taken from another boat and from a sea plane. Rather than slowing down the pace of the action though, these static shots greatly contribute to increase the sense of doom that dominates the film: for instance, when the Empusa makes its sombre entrance into Wisborg's harbour, the fact that we are watching it from a side-lined position and are not moving along with it to follow its trail, makes us feel even more overwhelmed by the fear and premonition of the terrible tragedy that is about to strike – our immobility as spectators replicating the helplessness of the citizens that will soon be hit by the plague brought on by the vampire. Alexandre Astruc wrote that '[…] with Murnau each image demands annihilation by another image. Every sequence announces its own end', there is a palpable sense of an encroaching and terrible outside world that bounces and reverberates between the images and the wider narrative of the film.[80]

Instead of being conveyed by camera movements, power relations and the characters' psychological states are often expressed through the use of angles. For instance, Murnau photographs the vampire taking over the ship using an extreme low angle that emphasises his power over mortals and renders the monster even more intimidating. In general, whenever Nosferatu is on screen, the weight of his commanding presence seems to dominate – or to 'colonise' and 'vampirise' as suggested by Ken Gelder – the surrounding space, regardless of the angle through which he is being framed.[81] As Eric Rhode wrote:

> […] when he emerges high on the edge of a horizon, or framed in a doorway, or walking the deck of a ship, he seems to take possession of these places and rob them of their identity. Coffins and doorways become apt niches for his emaciated body, and bare fields seem to distend from his gnarled form.[82]

At the opposite end of the scale the director films the vertiginous drop from Hutter's window in the castle from an extremely high angle that stresses the verticality of the castle's walls and by extension the character's desperate predicament and hopelessness in looking for a way out. For a fleeting second, we too are there with Hutter as he frantically looks around for an escape route. Murnau, who was clearly deeply aware of his technique, discussed on various occasions the nature of what his critics at times called 'a passion for camera angles'. For instance, in a passage quoted by Lotte Eisner in her biography of the director, he claims that

There should be no such thing as 'an interesting camera angle'. The angle in itself has no significance, and if it does not intensify the dramatic effect of the scene it can even be harmful. When you have the opportunity of seeing the rushes of a film every day, you are sometimes very enthusiastic at the time about certain shots that seem very clever. But afterwards, when you see the film as a whole, with all those so-called interesting camera angles, you realise they damage the action: they only lower, instead of intensifying, the dramatic interest of the story, because they are merely 'interesting' without having any dramatic value.[83]

What I think comes across very clearly from this quotation is how far removed Murnau was from the passion for unusual angles that characterises so strongly many Expressionist films. An impressive angle with no dramatic value has a very limited, and exclusively aesthetic, interest and the director stressed this idea yet again in 1928 when he wrote an article for the American women's magazine *McCall's* entitled 'Films of the Future' in which he discussed how he imagined the future of cinema. Amongst many interesting reflections on sound cinema, the advent of colour and the perfect silent drama that should dispense completely with intertitles, Murnau wrote:

They say I have a passion for 'camera angles'. But I do not take trick scenes from unusual positions just to get startling effects. To me the camera represents the eye of a person, through whose mind one is watching the events on the screen. It must follow characters at times into difficult places […] whirl and peep and move from place to place as swiftly as thought itself […] I think the films of the future will use more and more of these 'camera angles', or as I prefer to call them these 'dramatic angles.' They will help to photograph thought.[84]

In *Nosferatu* some of the most unnerving sequences are set up around very basic, straight-on but highly 'dramatic' angles – think, for example, of Orlok's first appearance in the castle's courtyard when the eye level shot gives us the impression of being directly scrutinised by his malevolent stare (see Figure 4) or when, thanks to the cross-cutting technique and the use of the same camera angle, Murnau establishes a direct connection between Orlok and Ellen despite the fact that the two characters are spatially separated (see for this Figures 6 and 7). What we are left with is the overwhelming impression that in Murnau's cinema 'feeling […] surpasses fact' and even the most apparently innocent shot can hide and convey an exceptional degree of disturbing intensity.[85]

The choice of angles in the film also has an impact on the degree of depth through which the scenes are photographed. From a general point of view, Nosferatu is a film devoid of shallow focus shots: the film's locations are usually filmed in deep focus and our eyes are free to roam around them looking for details and hidden meanings. The real horror in Nosferatu does not lie in what is unseen or in what can only be glimpsed at through blurred vision but can be found instead in the possibility of seeing things in such a sharp and unforgiving manner. This aesthetic choice is reflected onto the narrative: Ellen is tormented by the clear image of the vampire longing for her in the abandoned warehouse that is always shot in deep focus behind her bedroom's window. What she sees and what she senses, her acute feeling of being observed and stalked, become intertwined with her conscious research for an explanation that is provided in the film by her reading of the Book of Vampires. Observation and knowledge can often channel a sense of control over reality and we could therefore argue that it is exactly Ellen's capacity of 'seeing through' or 'seeing beyond' what is immediately apparent that makes her, on the one hand, more vulnerable to the vampire but on the other also the sole character who is capable of finding a way to destroy him.

One of the most important cinematographic aspects in the film can be found in the key role played by the use of light and shadow that are exploited in order to create a dialectic between reality and the world of darkness inhabited by the vampire and to transform into visuals the film's sombre Stimmung (mood). Nosferatu opens up on the everyday image of the city of Wisborg bathed in glorious sunshine: from the top of the tower where Murnau placed his camera – as he confesses in 'Films of the Future': '[…] I ask that they make me special equipment so that I can get my camera where I want it'[86] – we can observe the place going about its business, oblivious of the tragedy that is about to unfold. The extreme long shot that frames the diminutive citizens already appears to be stressing their vulnerability and fragility and our position as external observers seems to eerily anticipate somehow the famous opening sequence in Stanley Kubrick's The Shining (1980) during which we trail Jack Torrance's yellow VW Beetle from a detached perspective that Roger Luckhurst compares to that of malevolent gods toying with human faith.[87] From this point on, though, the film initiates a descent into darkness both narratively – through the staging of the vampiric plague that relentlessly kills anyone who crosses its path – and visually, since shadows are used in a prominent manner in many of the film's key events. Consider, for instance, Orlok's attack on Hutter, or the shadow theatre re-enacted at the climax of Knock's chase sequence or the scenes featuring Ellen's somnambulism and ultimate sacrifice.

Always beautifully photographed, Murnau's film is also enriched by the numerous intertextual references to art that are a direct result of the director's artistic sensibility and background studies in Art History first in Berlin and then at Heidelberg University. Some of these connections have already been mentioned in the close reading section of this book and there are also many scholars who have underlined and discussed this important aspect in *Nosferatu*. Amongst them, Angela Dalle Vacche has identified the wide range of references present in the film as oscillating between two polar opposites: that of Romantic painting – especially the works of Caspar David Friedrich that are recalled in many outdoors shots and in the recurrent use of the Rückenfigur – and that of modern Expressionist art – identified in the allusions to the works of Franz Marc, Arnold Böcklin, Edvard Munch and others. Dalle Vacche also underlines how these two groups of references, although perfectly integrated within the film and with each other, may not be the product of the same set of intentions:

> The allusions to Friedrich's paintings and Biedermeier décor must have been consciously planned by Murnau and his collaborators, who travelled to specific sites before shooting and worked from a script that included sketches of furniture. However, the links between *Nosferatu*'s apocalyptic view of the historical process and Marc's animal paintings or Munch's anguished vision of modernity may stem from the film itself, from its power to convey the climate of an age well beyond the immediate intentions of the director and his team.[88]

The frequent allusions to art serve a double purpose in the film. On the one hand, they achieve the practical result of reinforcing the impression of cultural prestige that was an important concern of Weimar filmmakers who strived to combine in their films their artistic sensibility with popular appeal and box-office potentiality. In years when cinema was still regarded by some – the guardians of the moral of differing religious and political orders – as immoral and corrupting, investing a film with a veneer of cultural respectability protected the work from possible attacks also improving at the same time the filmmakers' chances to obtain funds from potential sponsors and would-be producers. On the other hand, these hints create a continuity line that goes from the sense of supernatural wonder and longing often expressed in Romantic paintings and that feeling of horror for modern life and the unfulfilled desire to revert to a more human dimension that was enhanced by the shock caused by World War One and was conveyed by those Modernist movements, such as Die Brücke and Der Blaue Reiter, that are successfully conjured up in the film by means of its visual allusions.

For most of its narrative, *Nosferatu*'s plot unfolds in a linear fashion and we witness the events as they take place, discovering what is happening pretty much at the same time as the characters, although, as we have seen, thanks to the process of phasing we end up being able to put things together more quickly than, for instance, Hutter. The world recreated by the filmmakers is therefore a coherent universe that despite allowing for the existence of a supernatural dimension maintains and preserves the logical links between cause and effect. From a cinematographic point of view, this world is put on the screen through an editing style that follows the principles of classical continuity: the viewers are normally not expected to put together scattered pieces of action or to find their way around shots that can put out of balance their perception of space and time, for instance through the use of jump cuts or shots that contradict the 180-degree rule. The frequent employment of the iris in/out technique contributes in giving a sense of closure to the various segments of the plot that fade to black at the end of their narrative arch thus allowing for a smooth transition to another event, location, or time. There are however a few instances where Murnau shakes the linearity of his narration by experimenting with the technique of cross-cutting. Most notably, the director switches to this narrative mode in all the sequences that constitute crucial narrative turning points within the film's action. As we have already seen then, Orlok's attack on Hutter is intercut with Ellen's somnambulism whilst the vampire's voyage towards Wisborg is orchestrated as a piece of cinematic virtuosity when is cross-cut with four other narrative strands. Finally, the narrative climax of the film intertwines three storylines: Ellen waiting for Orlok in her bedroom, the vampire's shadow approaching along the stairs, and Hutter going to fetch Dr. Bulwer for help. Murnau's use of dramatic cross-cutting can be regarded as one of the most interesting features in the film and it fully validates the use of the word 'symphony' in the film's subtitle. The director's approach to the cross-cutting technique is also notable throughout the film because Murnau invests it with a series of complex and highly symbolic meanings that seem to anticipate the principles of Sergey Eisenstein's 'montage of attractions' (1923), an editing style focusing on

> […] any element […] that subjects the audience to emotional or psychological influence, verified by experience and mathematically calculated to produce specific emotional shocks in the spectator in their proper order within the whole. These shocks provide the only opportunity of perceiving the ideological aspect of what is being shown, the final ideological conclusion.[89]

If in a film like D.W. Griffith's *The Lonely Villa* (1909), to name just one example, the cross-cutting is used exclusively to produce narrative tension, in *Nosferatu* the various events, characters and sets are interlocked through a series of sinister correspondences and analogies that could appear to be shocking or somewhat inconsequential to a distracted eye (think for example of the use of the shadow of the vampire's hands that connects in a circular narration the attack on Hutter and Ellen's sacrifice) but that are in fact perfectly interconnected – even though they are not characterised by the overtly political and ideological imprint that strongly distinguishes Eisenstein's and more generally Soviet cinema in the 1920s from other kinds of narrative cinema. This all-encompassing approach to film editing, one that brings together narrative threads and deeper correspondences, has at the same time an anticipatory and intellectual quality: it brings the action forward by providing the film with a frantic pace, especially in the film's second half that is entirely sustained by the tension caused by Hutter's and Orlok's parallel rush to Wisborg. At the same time, though, simultaneous actions resonate at a deeper and visionary level by filling the narrative gaps that are inevitably created between events taking place in distant spaces and times.

4.2 INTERPRETATIONS

The visual and editorial complexities of *Nosferatu* presented in the last paragraph also had an impact on the numerous interpretations that have been attached to the film since its release in 1922. The sheer number of these interpretations and their great variety both in terms of focus and scope are a testimony to the ultimately elusive nature of the film and to its enduring vitality. With this paragraph, I aim to provide the readers with an overview – by no means exhaustive – of the film's most influential and interesting interpretations. At the same time though, I will avoid going too much into detail because it is not my intention to plainly reproduce here the critics' ideas and words that should instead be read and investigated in their entirety: consider this section as a starting point from where to begin the journey of discovery into the possible meanings hidden behind the film's visuals.

Some critics might argue that today, more than ninety years after the film's completion, *Nosferatu* may have lost some of its allure and that some of the elements constituting the film – for instance, the exaggerated acting style of some of its interpreters or the use of certain special effects such as the cranked-up motion of Orlok's carriage – may result old fashioned or even involuntarily comical. However, I would personally argue against this reading: it may be true that the performances of Alexander Granach or Gustav von Wangenheim may be overstated even by silent cinema standards and it may also be true that the film's special effects are rather simplistic compared to modern canons but it would be wrong to evaluate the film according to the 'scare-factor' we might expect or hope to get from a contemporary horror film. It would be wrong to let these details diminish the impact of the film that instead should be sought in the overall strength of its construction. The visionary imagination that can be glimpsed behind the way the story is developed onto the screen, the invention of the vampire itself as a frightening living corpse and the long series of aesthetic and narrative choices discussed in this volume still make the film genuinely chilling and animated by an undercurrent of tension that would be impossible to deny. As film critic Roger Ebert wrote:

> [The film] knows none of the later tricks of the trade, like sudden threats that pop in from the side of the screen. But *Nosferatu* remains effective: It doesn't scare us, but it haunts us. It shows not that vampires can jump out of shadows, but that evil can grow there, nourished on death.[90]

The initial responses to the film were generally positive. As we have seen previously, the German press reacted well to *Nosferatu* and appreciated its gloomy atmosphere and tragic darkness and the only voice rising against the film was that of the Marxist newspaper *Leipziger Volkszeitung* that lamented the film's descent into visual and narrative darkness by interpreting it as a refusal to engage with reality and politics. Even when the film was presented abroad either soon after its release or in the years immediately following it, its reception was overall a positive one. The French Surrealists, for instance, adored *Nosferatu* and regarded it as a prime example of 'liberating cinema' – a cinema that could free the mind from the shackles of reality and, by entering into the deepest recesses of the human mind, create a genuine dimension of the marvellous where imagination could have free rein. As already mentioned in a previous chapter, André Breton wrote about the film on two occasions in 1926 and 1932 but also other Surrealist artists and intellectuals celebrated *Nosferatu* in their writings. The poet Robert Desnos, for instance, wrote about it in three of his articles, one of which appeared in the Belgian newspaper *Le Soir* in 1927. In his article, Desnos conjured up the film using the kind of eerie and evocative language that was typical of Surrealist writing:

Perdu dans une forêt profonde dont le sol est fait de mousse et d'aiguilles de pin et dont la lumière est filtrée par les hauts eucalyptus [...] le voyageur moderne cherche le merveilleux. Il croit reconnaître le domaine promis à ses rêves par la nuit. Celle-ci tombe ténébreuse, pleine de mystère et de promesses. Un grand projecteur magique poursuit les créatures fabuleuses. Voici *Nosferatu* le Vampire [...].

[Lost in a deep forest where the soil is made of moss and pine needles and where the light is filtered by the tall eucalypti [...] the modern voyager is in search of the supernatural. He believes he recognises the land promised to his dreams by the night that falls on him, dark, full of mysteries and promises. A big magical searchlight hunts the fabulous creatures. Here comes *Nosferatu* the Vampire.][91]

If the Surrealists were able to naturally grasp the hidden significance of *Nosferatu*, more mainstream French critics appreciated the film at least on the basis of its technical merits and often compared it, although not necessarily in a favourable way, to that staple of France's popular theatre that was at the time the Théâtre du Grand Guignol, famous for its staging of horrific and gruesome plays.

Due to its problematic legal life, *Nosferatu* did not enjoy regular visibility in the years immediately after its completion and serious readings of the film only started after the end of the Second World War when the copy preserved at the Cinémathèque Française in Paris finally resurfaced. This finding, along with a more generalised interest in German cinema, gave the opportunity to several critics and scholars to start analysing the films produced during the Weimar Republic as a means to find an answer or an explanation to the dictatorial drift that had brought Germany and the rest of the world on the brink of annihilation. As a consequence, post-war readings of the film immediately took on a much darker tone.

The first major study to discuss the film was published by the German critic and social scientist Siegfried Kracauer in 1947. Associated with the Frankfurt School, Kracauer considered cinema as a good indicator to study major changes in society. In other words, due to their complex nature straddling the line between art and business enterprise seeking popular approval, films could encode and transmit new ideas and attitudes that could mirror, influence or shape social shifts. Kracauer's study entitled *From Caligari to Hitler. A Psychological History of the German Film* is based on the central assumption, already clearly expressed in the book's title, that the films produced during the years of the Weimar Republic encrypted and passed on a series of disturbing hidden ideas that ultimately contributed to the success of the National Socialist Party. Amongst these ideas, Kracauer analyses the desire to retreat from reality – embodied, for instance, by the artificially reconstructed sets typical of Expressionist cinema or the fatalism and mental confusion that characterised Germany in the years following the end of World War One and that resulted in a series of films constructed around narratives steeped in a fantasy world often populated by doppelgängers or highly contrasting figures that brought onto the screen the ultimate political dilemma between conservatism and revolution that stirred the country between 1918 and 1933. In Kracauer's words:

> The German soul, haunted by the alternative images of tyrannic rule and instinct-governed chaos, threatened by doom on either side, tossed about in gloomy space like the phantom ship in *Nosferatu*.[92]

The indecision between order and chaos faced by the German people is thus connected by Kracauer to the considerable number of films featuring a tyrannical character in their narrative. *The Cabinet of Dr. Caligari* is considered as a prime example of these films 'specialized in the depiction of tyrants'[93] and is thus discussed at length in the book. Kracauer, however, also analyses other films that he considers to be characterised by the same attitude and *Nosferatu* – along with *Vanina* (Arthur Von Gerlach, 1922) and *Dr. Mabuse, der Spieler* – is amongst them. In his interpretation of the film, the vampire is decoded as a tyrannical figure that can be seen to stand as a metaphor for the hyperinflation that in the 1920s was quite literally sucking the blood out of the Germans' finances. The vampire inflicts pain and suffering to whomever crosses his path and his predominance is hardly ever challenged; Hutter, Bulwer and the other characters are either incapable or strangely unwilling to contrast him. The only person who can face the challenge is the virginally pure Ellen that manages to destroy the monster only through the supernatural power of her love. The closing of *Nosferatu*'s narrative is thus explained by Kracauer as a clear example of that retreat from reality that characterised the Weimar Republic: Germany's social and financial crisis cannot be resolved through political actions but only by means of a wish-fulfilment fantasy, a miracle that will make society's evils disappear magically in a cloud of white smoke – or by extension in a sea of swastika flags. This interpretation of *Nosferatu* contributed to create the idea that the film could be read as an endorsement of the anti-Semitic attacks that right wing political groups, especially the National Socialists, conducted in the years of the Weimar Republic against the Jewish community that was considered to be responsible for Germany's defeat in the war through the spreading of the so-called 'stab in the back' myth: the idea that Jews, along with socialists and communists, had not supported the war effort but had instead betrayed their own country by selling Germany to its enemies. According to this interpretation then, Count Orlok should be seen as the personification of the Jew taking advantage of Germany's social, financial and political disarray whilst Ellen could be read as the embodiment of the resilience and purity of real German values that are finally triumphant even through sacrifice. This reading of the film also echoes a rather common interpretation of Bram Stoker's *Dracula* that sees the vampire as the symbol of a wave of reverse colonisation that threatened from the East the values of Victorian England. Furthermore, some of the physical features of Count Orlok could be seen as a give-away to further endorse this interpretation.

The anti-Jewish image, disseminated by every single party and movement on the right, became […] virulent in the 1920s. Jews were inevitably hunchbacked, long-bearded, malevolent-looking. Their noses were stereotypically big; their eyes peered out from sunken sockets with a malicious gaze. Their limbs, more tentacles than arms and legs, spread over the earth or their unsuspecting victims [...].[94]

The hooked nose, the spidery limbs, the sunken eyes are all features that we can identify in the film's depiction of the vampire, however, other elements, the really prominent ones such as the long beard and the hunchback, are missing from the character's mise-en-scène. In any case, the presence of these visual traits is hardly enough to justify such a radical interpretation of the film that also seems to be contradicted by other, more biographical, elements. We know for example that Murnau was not a political radical and that he had long-standing and friendly relationships with many Jewish individuals: his lover Hans Ehrenbaum-Degele came from a prominent Jewish family that practically adopted Murnau after Hans' death in the trenches and also Alexander Granach, who had known Murnau since the days spent together in Max Reinhardt's Deutsches Theater, confirmed in his autobiography the director's lack of anti-Semitic sentiments:

In his memoirs Granach tells how Murnau, always chivalrous, defended him, a little Jew from Galicia, whose German was still imperfect, from the anti-Semitic attacks of Professor Held [...].[95]

Finally, when the film came out no one underlined, praised or criticised a possible anti-Semitic interpretation of the film that even appears to demonstrate, especially towards the end of its narrative arch, a certain degree of sympathy for the vampire's pitiful isolation.

Although still fascinating and very influential, Kracauer's study of Weimar cinema has at times been criticised for the tightness of its scope and for its forced reading of the films discussed that are analysed in a sort of ex-post fashion: already having clear and well-established arguments in mind, Kracauer looks for confirmation in the films by explaining them in his own terms that do not leave much space to any real discussion of the features' cinematographic specificities. Of course, reading a film from a socio-political perspective is a perfectly viable option but some interpretations stemming from Kracauer's work appear to have further narrowed down the scope of their reading thus reducing the film's complexity to simple one-dimensional schemes that do not take into serious account the layered mechanics behind film production and social shifts. The most successful sociological interpretations of *Nosferatu* are therefore those that have managed to apply to the film a framework that put into relation cinema and society while at the same time taking into consideration the specific aspects of filmmaking, both in terms of aesthetics and production process. From this point of view, it is particularly interesting to take into consideration Anton Kaes' reading of Weimar cinema as an example of shell-shocked cinema that manages to translate onto the screen that sense of trauma and disruption suffered by Germany after the traumatic events of World War One.[96] Through his interpretation Kaes sees *Nosferatu* as a metaphor of the lost generation of 1914 and turns it into a radical piece of criticism directed against German conservative and military elites.

> [...] the film takes recourse to vampire lore to narrate the war experience: for Murnau, the vampire's need for blood and his ruthless victimization of innocence connotes the nature of war. In *Nosferatu*, Hutter's story parallels that of a soldier from the lost generation, while his equally traumatized wife, Ellen, embodies the home front living in fear and gripped by a death wish. [...] Count Orlok [...] (whose name is evocative of *oorlog*, the Dutch word for 'war'), invades the town and brings mass death with him. The killing does not stop until a young woman sacrifices herself for the community. A lost generation indeed.[97]

There are also several other studies (Wood, 1970, or Sklar, 1993) that have analysed *Nosferatu* by interweaving the film's cinematic characters either into a more or less ample social metaphor or along the lines of a psychological or psychoanalytical reading: the film, and especially the central character of Ellen and the ambiguous love triangle between her, Hutter and Orlok have been scrutinised from a feminist perspective or discussed in terms of a complex analysis of human desires. Thus in some interpretations, such as that by Jo Leslie Collier,[98] Ellen becomes the embodiment of the Romantic ideal of the 'asexual madonna', a woman regarded as a Higher Being, wholly unattainable by man on a physical level but thoroughly desirable on an ideological one. Burdened with the heavy inheritance of Romanticism's idealised woman, Murnau decides to challenge it by breaking its mould and creating a female heroine who is ready to resist and go against the role traditionally assigned to her, for instance by consciously breaking Hutter's prohibition to read the *Book of Vampires*:

One structure that can be abstracted from the various Murnau narratives is the attempt by the male and/or society to impose the romantic ideal on the female and her resistance to such an imposition. The Murnau woman wants to shed the halo that has been thrust upon her and regain her position as active and co-equal sexual partner.[99]

Collier also connects Murnau's construction of her rebellious female characters – not exclusively of *Nosferatu*'s Ellen – to the director's covert criticism of German society's suppression of the homosexual subject who was forced to live in a repressive society that still applied Paragraph 175, a law provision created in 1871 that considered sexual acts between males as a crime and appealed to 'the people's consciousness of right and wrong [to condemn] these activities not merely as vice but also as a crime',[100] and that by 1924 had brought to prison about seven hundred people.[101] Other scholars, such as Stan Brakhage, have favoured an analytical approach that attempted to find in the film clues about Murnau's sexual orientation and it would be thus possible to read the figure of the vampire and his interaction with Hutter as a codified and hidden representation of homosexual subjects and relations. Besides, as underlined by Harry M. Benshoff: '[…] homosexuals, like vampires, have rarely cast a reflection in the social looking-glass of popular culture' and horror cinema – by its very nature already centred on a perversion of normality – can easily be read in queer terms that identify the monster living at the margins of society with the rejected homosexual subject.[102]

Along with Kracauer's book, the other influential post-war study of Weimar cinema was certainly *The Haunted Screen: Expressionism in German Cinema* published in 1969 by Lotte Eisner who also published important biographies of F.W. Murnau and Fritz Lang. Eisner worked as Chief Archivist at the Cinémathèque Française from 1945 to 1975 thus having privileged access to the films preserved there under the directorship of Henri Langlois. Lotte Eisner's approach was essentially stylistic and was profoundly shaped by her idea of 'influence' that saw Weimar cinema and Expressionism as a product of the artistic, literary and theatrical seeds planted in German culture from the Romantic movement of the 1820s onwards. Throughout her study then, she proceeds to construct a dense web of intertextual references that have the ultimate aim to prove the existence of a sense of continuity in Germany's aesthetic sensibility. Eisner's book is certainly a fascinating study and to this day, it can still be considered an important source book for the sensitivity she demonstrates in handling the mutations undergone by Romanticism once it entered the realm of the moving pictures.[103] If Kracauer avoided discussing the visual complexities of the films under analysis, Eisner's approach is completely opposite: her book, also enriched by a wealth of fascinating stills and pictures, examines the lighting, texture and composition of the films in great depth: *Nosferatu* is particularly praised for the majestic beauty of its shots which are described with lyrical terms that testify to Eisner's intense admiration for Murnau, who is unmistakably identified as a genius. Rather interestingly, Eisner also proceeds in establishing a tentative connection between Murnau's evocative and painterly cinematography and the Scandinavian cinema of the 1910s that presented in the works of directors such as Viktor Sjöström, Benjamin Christensen, Mauritz Stiller and others a profound interest for outdoor realism and the poetic treatment of nature that can be also found in *Nosferatu* and in other films by the German director:

> Murnau was one of the few German film directors to have the innate love for landscape more typical of the Swedes [...] and he was always reluctant to resort to artifice.[104]

The marked variations discernible within Murnau's body of works, and his difference when compared to other Expressionist filmmakers, is at least partially attributed by Eisner to the director's sexual orientation that she considers to be at the core of his existential malaise. In Eisner's words:

> Murnau had homosexual tendencies. In his attempt to escape from himself, he did not express himself with the artistic continuity which makes it so easy to analyse the style of, say, Lang. [...] all his films bear the impress of his inner complexity, of the struggle he waged within himself against a world in which he remained despairingly alien.[105]

Although certainly fascinating, however, Eisner's interpretation of Weimar cinema seems to suffer from the same limitations of Kracauer's study; her approach is incredibly single-minded and if Kracauer aims to demonstrate the connection between Weimar films and the Nazi dictatorship, she tries to build up a continuity line from Romanticism to Expressionism that results at times somewhat mechanical. As underlined by Thomas Elsaesser, who has recently published a study that tries to provide a new and fresh interpretation of Weimar cinema:

[Kracauer's and Eisner's] works [...] have encouraged a potent analogy between film culture and political history, where experience (of key films) so uncannily matches expectation (of what German cinema should 'reflect') that the convergence of image with its object has for nearly fifty years seemed all but self-evident.[106]

It would be important therefore to shake off preconceived ideas and interpretations in order to try and read the film with fresh eyes that could on the one hand establish connections either with society or art while on the other maintain a clear and respectful view of *Nosferatu*'s cinematographic specificities. This is the real challenge for whoever embarks on an interpretative exercise of such a rich and elusive film.

CHAPTER 5 – *NOSFERATU'S* AFTERLIVES

Nosferatu or at least some of the film's most iconic images such as the nightmarish vision of the pale and lanky vampire popping up from a coffin or his long, spidery hands crawling along the walls of Ellen's home are undoubtedly embedded in popular culture and are thus often quoted.

For instance, in Francis Ford Coppola's *Bram Stoker's Dracula* (1992) Gary Oldman's shadow seems to be endorsed with a materiality and a life of its own that is reminiscent of the portentous shadow projected by Count Orlok in *Nosferatu*. Murnau's film has also been parodied: the BBC sketch programme *The Fast Show* (1994-1997), for instance, featured the recurrent character of a vampire that looked very similar to Orlok who creeps up to a sleeping woman not to drink her blood but to give her betting advice. The film has also been reprised and quoted innumerable times; think for example of the bluish and repulsive Mr Barlow, the terrifying vampire featured in the television adaptation of Stephen King's *Salem's Lot* (1979).

Its impact is not simply limited to cinema or television: there are comics books featuring Nosferatu as their villain or main character but also operas and rock songs that more or less directly refer to the character. Finding all the references and homages can be a fascinating and amusing journey into the depths of art, pop culture and fan fiction. It is not, however, within the scope of this book to provide the reader with an exhaustive list of all the Count's reincarnations. Nevertheless, all these quotations, parodies and allusions, although differing from the point of view of quality and artistry, are important in their own right because they act as an everlasting testimony to the vitality and ultimate immortality of the imaginary world that has accompanied the film since its release in 1922. In this final chapter of my study I intend to outline briefly two cinematic reprisals and reworkings of the original film: Werner Herzog's *Nosferatu Phantom der Nacht* released in 1979 that can be considered as a legitimate remake of Murnau's film, and the biopic/making of/vampire flick *Shadow of the Vampire* directed by E. Elias Merhige in 2000.

5.1 BETWEEN TRIBUTE AND ALIENATION: HERZOG'S
NOSFERATU PHANTOM DER NACHT

Werner Herzog directed his vampire film in 1979. *Nosferatu Phantom der Nacht*, distributed in English-speaking countries as *Nosferatu the Vampyre*, cannot be regarded simply as another adaptation of Bram Stoker's *Dracula* but it is first and foremost a narratively complex and visually thought-provoking remake and revision of Murnau's original film. By the end of the 1970s the original novel, published in 1897, had entered into the public domain and Herzog, who also wrote the film's script, re-adapted the book by implementing some changes that connected it more directly and unequivocally to its literary roots. The repossession of the literary origins of *Dracula*, however, was not necessarily extended to all the narrative details of Herzog's film that is characterised in fact by an intriguing mixture of loyalties and departures both from its literary and cinematic sources.

When we compare *Phantom der Nacht* with the film made in 1922, the most evident of the changes implemented by the director is the reverting of the characters' names – changed in Murnau's film because of the copyright issues already outlined in this study – to their original versions. In Herzog's reworking therefore there is Count Dracula (Klaus Kinski) haunting the lives of Jonathan Harker (Bruno Ganz) and his wife Lucy (Isabelle Adjani) who replaces Mina as the female heroine in the story. We also have the characters of Renfield (Roland Topor), who embodies again the functions of Harker's employer and Dracula's first slave, and that of Dr Van Helsing who, although by all means not restored in its literary centrality, will be the one to make sure that the vampire is dead at the end of the film by putting a stake through his heart after Lucy's ultimate sacrifice. Herzog also restored a couple of Dracula's iconic speeches in his version of the film, such as the mention of the 'children of the night' or the one about the nobility of Dracula's race. More generally, his vampire is characterised by a willingness to share his existential anguish with the viewer who slowly comes to realise that Dracula, unlike Orlok who is driven exclusively by his physical need for blood, has retained a certain degree of inner life and is suffering because of his undead condition that has forced him to endure century upon century of *Nichtigkeiten*, the emptiness and meaninglessness of human life protracted well beyond its natural limits. This sense of emotional unrest brings Herzog's creation somewhat closer to its literary ancestor who speculates at times in the novel about the glorious experience of real death as integral to what constitutes humanity. In the novel's second chapter, for instance, Dracula declares:

> I long to go through the crowded streets of your mighty London, to be in the midst of the whirl and rush of humanity, to share its life, its change, its death, and all that makes it what it is.[107]

Despite these proximities with the original novel, the core of Herzog's interests remains firmly in Murnau's work. In terms of narrative loyalty to its cinematic antecedent, Herzog's film, just like Murnau's, is set in Wismar in the early part of the nineteenth century and revolves around a plot that roughly follows that of the 1922 film rather than the novel's. The overall structure of the original *Nosferatu* is preserved, for example, through the employment of cross-cutting to build up narrative tension and the psychic links that connect the three main characters in the film, which are also reinforced through visual clues such as the contiguous shots that frame Dracula and Lucy advancing in Wismar's central square both enveloped in long, flowing black cloaks.

Figure 13 Dracula taking possession of Wismar

There are, however, some significant details that have been changed by Herzog and that touch both the construction of the characters' psychology, such as Dracula's existential weariness or Lucy's sexual attractiveness, and the actual events featured in the film. [Fig.

Figure 14 Lucy following Dracula's steps

From this point of view, it is essential to mention at least the radical departure from Murnau's work in the film's ending when we ultimately discover that Lucy's sacrifice has been pointless and that Jonathan has been turned into a vampire and is now ready to ride off to spread un-death and plague into the world. This dismal ending has often been interpreted as a serious variant of the final sequence in Roman Polanski's *Dance of the Vampires* (1967) where the two main characters, Sarah (Sharon Tate) and Alfred (Roman Polanski) are turned into vampires at the end of the film.[108] As underlined by S.S. Prawer in his insightful study of Herzog's film:

> [In] Murnau's world […] redemption comes through the love and self-sacrifice of a woman 'pure of heart'. Herzog's [world] is more akin to that of Don Siegel's *Invasion of the Body Snatchers* (1955), whose ending is recalled when Lucy tries frantically to tell her fellow citizens that she knows where the evil comes from and how it can be fought, only to be told to go home, for there was nothing to be done. […] The citizens […] in Herzog's film push Lucy aside as they go on ceremoniously carrying the coffins of those whom they are shortly bound to join.[109]

By means of an uncomfortably prolonged closing shot the spectator of Herzog's film is left with a sense of impending darkness and doom that cannot be retraced in Murnau's film that, although ending on a note of sadness because of Ellen's death, also presents a restoration of the natural order through the dispatching of the vampire and 'the victorious radiance of the living sun'.

5.2 THE ARTIST AS DESPOT: MERHIGE'S SHADOW OF THE VAMPIRE

If Werner Herzog's *Nosferatu Phantom der Nacht* can be regarded as a tribute and remake of Murnau's original, E. Elias Merhige's *Shadow of the Vampire* (2000) is a fascinating hybrid that combines biographical cinema and backstage drama with the tropes of traditional vampire film while at the same time commenting and analysing ideas such as that of the vampire as a cinematographic construct, and that of cinema's inner nature as being equivalent to some kind of parasitic vampire. Before moving on to a necessarily contained analysis of the film's main points, I would like to add that *Shadow of the Vampire* has a special place in my list of favourite vampire films and that I was very fortunate to have the chance, while working on this book, to interview Elias Merhige who has provided me with some insightful ideas about his work. The following paragraphs will draw some material from our interview that can be read in its entirety as an appendix to this study.

The story of *Shadow of the Vampire* revolves around a very simple plot twist based on an urban legend that has long accompanied Murnau's film: namely the rumour that Max Schreck, the actor interpreting Orlok, was in fact a real vampire. This far-fetched yet captivating idea – also reinforced by the fact that the word 'Schreck' can be translated from German with 'terror' or 'fright', thus sounding like the perfect *nom de plume* for an actor playing a demonic vampire in a horror film – was first launched by the Greek filmmaker and writer Ado Kyrou who, in his book *Le Surréalisme au cinéma* (1953), writes:

> In the role of the vampire the credits name the music-hall actor Max Schreck, but it is well-known that this attribution is a deliberate cover-up… No-one has ever been willing to reveal the identity of the extraordinary actor whom brilliant make-up renders absolutely unrecognisable. There have been several guesses, some even

mentioning Murnau… Who hides behind the character of *Nosferatu*? Maybe *Nosferatu* himself?[110]

It is moving from this premise that Steven Katz wrote the first draft of *Shadow of the Vampire*. The transformation of the initial idea into a finished film caused some artistic friction between Katz and Merhige who had rather diverging opinions on how the movie should be made and what should be its main narrative concern. In Katz's words:

> The director [and I] used to fight like hell when I'd say it was a vampire movie, and he'd say, 'No, it's not.' So when they started shooting it, he and producer Nic Cage, with a lot of influence from John Malkovich [...] shifted the thrust of the movie. I had originally wanted it to be just a really great vampire flick [...] But they stripped away a lot of the layers of horror I had and made [...] an art film about the nature of creativity and the relationship between the director and his film, which I had in the script, but as subtext only.[111]

Despite Katz's bitterness in recalling his experience, it is indeed the removal of the most obvious layers of traditional vampire horror – the 'glowing blue eyes' mentioned by Merhige in his interview – that contribute decisively to the complex and clever nature of *Shadow of the Vampire* that instead of playing along with the genre's topoi, tries to overturn them by focusing on the interplay between reality and fiction whose confines are blurred from the very beginning of the film.

Shadow of the Vampire opens with a series of contextualising intertitles – 'Jofa Film Studios. Berlin 1921', etc. – that ground the film in the reality of actual places and events. The intertitles are then followed by the contiguous extreme close-ups of what we will discover to be Murnau's eye and his camera lens: the quasi-superimposition between human and mechanical eye will be central for the development of Murnau's obsessive character in the film - 'If it's not in frame, it doesn't exist', he will declare towards the climax of the story - and appears here to be almost suggestive of Dziga Vertov's concept of the Kino-Glaz (Film-Eye) and reminiscent of its role in perfecting the inadequacy of reality as seen through the flawed human eye:

> I am kino-eye, I am a mechanical eye. I, a machine, show you the world as only I can see it. Now and forever, I free myself from human immobility [...].[112]

The focus on realism purported at the beginning of the film is apparently confirmed by its second sequence that presents the viewer with the recreation of the cinematographic set where Murnau (John Malkovich) and his crew are filming the opening sequence of Nosferatu. The experience of early filmmaking is re-established in the movie with great precision: Murnau and his assistants are all wearing long white lab coats and dark goggles, the transition between sequences is frequently signalled by iris shots and the whirring of the hand-cranked cameras can often be heard in the background of the film.

Figure 15 Creating enduring cinematographic memories

However, the simple narrative line of the 'film about the making-of of another film', visually presented also through the constant switching between B&W and colour photography, is complicated by the use of metafictional devices to remind us that what we are seeing on the screen is the fictional recreation about the realisation of another piece of fictional narrative. This metanarrative approach is further complicated by the twist on the character of the vampire played by Willem Dafoe:

> As soon as we find ourselves caught up in the circle of contemplating a 'real' actor (Dafoe) playing a vampire (Count Orlok) playing a human (Max Schreck) playing a vampire (Count Orlok), we've already been interpolated into Shadow of the Vampire's playful structure of meaning - its interrogation of the theatricality of the vampire

genre and the cinema's role in producing the vampires it endlessly pursues and destroys.[113]

Already in its first few minutes *Shadow of the Vampire* succeeds in presenting to the viewer many of its central issues: Murnau comes across as a despotic personality ready to manipulate his crew and actors into doing what he wants. For instance, he convinces Greta Schroeder (Catherine McCormack), who has reservations about cinematic acting and would much rather act in a theatrical play, that her role in the film will make her great as an actress and her absence from Berlin will be nothing more than a 'sacrifice for [her] art', a line that creepily foreshadows the tragic destiny that will await her at the end of the film. Murnau's obsession for realistic performance, and his dislike for the 'artifice' of in-studio reconstructions, is in line with his belief that cinema can act as a bridge between life and death, memory and oblivion, light and darkness. During a speech superimposed on the images of the train, aptly named Charon, that is transporting the film's crew on location, Murnau proclaims the manifesto of his new cinematographic art:

> Our art […] will have a context as certain as the grave. We are scientists engaged in the creation of memory. But our memory will neither blur nor fade.

The reference to filmmakers as scientists alludes to the perception of cinema as being halfway between science and entertainment that was still common in the early 1920s. On the other hand, though, it could be interpreted as a subtle nod to the long series of mad scientists that have animated the cinematographic screens in their attempts to achieve immortality or restore life.

Most importantly though, Murnau's obsession for 'undead' memories is at the basis of the fiendish pact that he strikes with Orlok who will pretend to be a method actor – 'one of the Russian school' – in exchange for the life of Greta Schroeder. The vampire acts in the film as a double of Murnau: in their own, peculiar way, Murnau through the camera and Orlok by means of his vampiric fangs, they both drain the life of those surrounding them in order to achieve immortality. Across the narrative arc of the film, though, their roles get reversed and we end up seeing Orlok as being more 'human' and sympathetic than Murnau who, in his Promethean effort to transcend the limits of mortality, unblinkingly sacrifices the lives of many of his crewmembers. In their exchanges Orlok taunts Murnau by underlining the basic similarity of their nature.

Orlok, however, appears to endure his undead condition with increasing weariness. In a way similar to Klaus Kinski's vampire in Werner Herzog's film, the vampire in Merhige's movie resents his immortality and his eternal condemnation to remain an old man and expresses his existential frustration in one of the most intense sequences in the film by reciting a short extract from a poem by Alfred Tennyson that retells the mythological story of Tithonus, the lover of Eos who manages to obtain from Zeus immortality for her companion but forgets to ask for his eternal youth:

> But thy strong Hours indignant work'd their wills,
> And beat me down and marr'd and wasted me,
> And tho' they could not end me, left me maim'd
> To dwell in presence of immortal youth,
> Immortal age beside immortal youth,
> And all I was, in ashes.[114]

At the end of the film, Orlok will be finally released from his undead prison and will disappear from the screen consumed by light, the only factor that can destroy both the vampire's and the cinematic image's illusion of immortality.

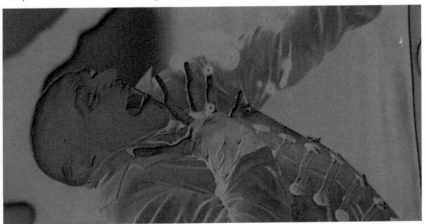

Figure 16 The vampire and the cinematic image consumed by light

Over the course of the months I have spent working on this book, *Nosferatu* has been very active. New publications, cinematographic retrospectives, and exhibitions have kept alive the Gothic imagination that accompanies the film and have injected new energy into the many questions it still raises on the inner nature of cinema and the enduring fascination for what may be hiding in the darkest recesses of the movie screen. As pointed out by Thomas Elsaesser:

> […] the excess energy of the undead is now readable as belonging to the cinema and its eccentric patterns of propagation and proliferation across the culture at large. Not only in the way films have deposited their coffins in galleries, museums, schools and libraries, but also thanks to the Renfields - cinephiles turned necrophiles - at home in archives, lovingly restoring perished prints and reviving the 'originals' at Sunday matiness or special retrospectives.[115]

Nosferatu is still with us.

APPENDIX: INTERVIEW WITH E. ELIAS MERHIGE

Q. How did *Shadow of the Vampire* come to be? Had it been a long-standing project for you?

A. *Shadow of the Vampire* came to me through actor Nicolas Cage who had started his own production company called Saturn Films, a detail that I found to be most curious because Albin Grau, the original producer of *Nosferatu*, published an esoteric journal from 1925 to 1929 titled 'Saturn Gnosis'. Personally, I found the sympathy of 'Saturn' as a reigning planetary force behind both *Nosferatu* and this mysterious script *Shadow of the Vampire* to be an uncanny association to say the least.

The history with Nicolas Cage and me is that he had been given a copy of my first movie *Begotten* (1991) as a present from either his wife or a friend and once he had seen it, he could not get this film out of his mind. When he created Saturn Film he used *Begotten* as an example, a template for the kind of filmmakers he would like to work with. After meeting with Nic's producing associate Jeff Levine, Saturn Films sent over a first draft of *Shadow of the Vampire* written by Steven Katz. At first, when I met with Saturn Films Nic was very excited with my vision for this film and said: 'I really want to see the film that is in your head.'

Q. How did you conceive your two main characters?

A. I wanted to explore the idea of the artist as 'despot', the director as a Promethean figure that will transgress and will stop at nothing in order to create something that will transcend his mortality and live forever in the culture of Humankind. I wanted my fictional version of Murnau to start out 'human' and become more and more of a monster as the story progressed and unravelled towards its conclusion in the final scene where we see the true 'artist-as-monster' reveal himself. We start *Shadow of the Vampire* with Murnau as a man, a film director, who sheds his humanity the deeper into the creative process he goes. He gets 'lost' in his own desire to create something so great that he manipulates and lies to his entire film crew deliberately keeping them in the 'dark' as to what his true intention is in making his film *Nosferatu*. As you follow the film and Murnau's story arc in *Shadow of the Vampire* you see less and less a man in John

Malkovich's character and more and more a manipulative beast that will stop at nothing to get his film made and finished.

Now, Schreck, the vampire character played by Willem Dafoe, is of an entirely different nature. When he first appears on screen in *Shadow of the Vampire*, we clearly are chilled by his presence and our blood runs cold as he looms out of the dark hole, like a tunnel of the castle, to greet Hutter played by Eddie Izzard. Schreck's arc in *Shadow of the Vampire* was to begin as a 'monster' and end as a 'human'. Schreck becomes more 'human' as we see him interacting with the crew and struggling like a child to find both acceptance and love and truth from both his director and from the scenes he is to partake in. I wanted for the audience to feel that Schreck was more human and Murnau less human in the end; to trade places in a sense where the director begins as man and ends as monster and the monster begins as monster and ends fragile and all too human.

Also I wanted it ambiguous as to whether Schreck is in fact a real vampire. I wanted to leave the audience thinking he is either a real vampire OR a totally obsessed actor that has 'become' the monster he is hired to portray. The original screenplay was not conceived like this. The characters were more clearly defined in the sense that you come to realise that Schreck is a real vampire and that Murnau has a moral compass and is protective of his crew when things get out of hand. There were more traditional tropes of the vampire genre in the original first draft of the screenplay. And this I wanted to remove from the story. It was far more interesting to me to play with the idea of 'artist as vampire' rather than 'vampire as vampire'.

Q. Were then significant differences between your ideas and Steven Katz's script?

A. Yes, yes, yes. The original script was very much in keeping with the genre of the vampire film and I did not want to follow this line of aesthetic in both story telling and content. I mean, if you have an opportunity to turn a genre on its head and break the rules of a genre, then why not go for it. In Katz's script there were moments when the vampire is looking at Greta from off stage and his eyes 'glow blue'. With a gesture like this, suddenly it takes any guessing away. Obviously if Schreck's eyes glow blue he is a supernatural figure and not a man. So he is not human and this creates a wall, a barrier in the audience that for me makes his character less complex, less layered and in a sense less interesting. It was important for me to present Schreck when he first appears to be undeniably a monster and then to follow his enigmatic presence and to reveal his fragility and his unquenchable desires and loss of memory as something that appears more human as the story evolves. This to me is the Human Vampire that I wanted to show in Willem Dafoe's characterisation of Schreck.

Q. In *Shadow of the Vampire* the contrast between progress and tradition, for instance portrayed in the clash between cinema and theatre represented by Murnau and Greta in the film's opening sequence, is a very strong recurrent theme. Would you agree?

A. Ah, yes. I am obsessed by the end of the Enlightenment and how with it you have the discovery of the unconscious hand in hand with the birth of psychoanalysis and all happening side by side with the birth of the motion picture camera. Swiftly, painting is replaced by the novelty of photography as portraiture and with the persistence of vision created by the motion picture projector. The 'still' photograph is given motion. If you look at the history of the cinema, it began in nickelodeons and peep shows where men could view women stripping off their clothing. Cinema began with an unseemly and audiences were highly suspicious exercising a kind of fear and reservation towards its engrossing power. There is a famous anecdote from a theatre in 1906 that showed a short movie depicting a train coming into its station. It was reported that as the train pulled in people cowered in their seats as if the train were in front of them in their seats. If cinema was the demonic bastard child, then theatre was for sure its angelic legitimate form of art.

Murnau never successfully obtained the rights from the Stoker family to film *Dracula* and so, under the banner of his new film company that he shared with Albin Grau, they changed the name to *Nosferatu*. The Stoker family thought it vulgar and unseemly that a film should be made from *Dracula*. Their main interest was seeing it as a theatrical play in London. What is interesting here is that Murnau who has begun his career as an artist in theatre saw the future of movies as the dominant art form of the twentieth century. There are a lot of references in *Shadow of the Vampire* to the camera as a demonic force that takes life in order to preserve it and in preserving it life becomes embalmed, a dead thing that exists only in shadows. There are references also, that Murnau makes in *Shadow of the Vampire* that the camera is the key to immortalising our temporary state as living beings. He calls the cinema the new cave upon which man paints his dreams and that the movies are the cave painting of the twentieth century. I find it very interesting in my own experiences as a film director when I see one of my actors staring with their complete attention into the camera performing for a completely dead thing. I contrast this with the theatre where my actors address a living audience whose camera is living eyes that record the experience of the drama and biology of their living memories. I find it interesting in the twenty-first century that whenever I go to a performance, musical or theatrical, there are so many younger members of the audience recording a theatrical event on their smartphone. I find it prescient that their eyes are on the screen of their smartphone, not on the stage. The virtual reality has become more dominant over actual reality.

Q. Due to its very nature, cinema bears a series of striking parallels with vampirism. Was this aspect a relevant element in *Shadow of the Vampire*?

A. Yes. Greta in the beginning of *Shadow of the Vampire* expresses her displeasure over the motion picture camera by saying to Murnau, '[…] the theatre audience gives me life, while this THING (pointing to the motion picture camera) takes it from me.' I've always been fascinated with the camera as some kind of divine and magical device that both steals and immortalises our struggle as dying creatures.

Q. How did you select and use the extracts from Murnau's film that found their way into *Shadow of the Vampire*?

A. When Hutter meets Nosferatu for the first time, I wanted to recreate Hutter's approach to the gate, his hesitation, his trepidation, his repression of abject fear. This transgression through this gate into the home of *Nosferatu* represented my transgression into Murnau's original movie and that was the bridge between the historical *Nosferatu* movie and my recreation. I am reopening the gate to Nosferatu a second time so that I may reveal another aspect, an alternate one that I hope will somehow deepen the way we view Murnau's *Nosferatu*. I am reopening the gate like the detective in my search to find the 'true vampire'.

I have recreated the scene of Hutter waking up in the morning in Nosferatu's castle having been scared the night before by the world of shadows and being falsely reassured by the light of day. There is brilliant humour to it, there is something beautiful about an excess of optimism in the face of death. Towards the end of the movie, I chose to recreate the scene where Greta laying in the bed has her heart squeezed by the shadow of Nosferatu's hand as a prelude to her character's actual death in my film. Art imitates life in this last scene of *Shadow of the Vampire*. In *Shadow of the Vampire* I made Greta's sacrifice literal, removing all metaphor. In the original *Nosferatu* it is the metaphor of Greta's pure heart that vanquishes the vampire, in *Shadow of the Vampire* it is Greta's opium rich blood that leads to the death of the vampire.

One of the most important recreations that follows is Nosferatu's death scene as he is exposed to the sunlight in the original *Nosferatu*, but in my film it is not only sunlight that kills, it is the lamp of the motion picture projector. This scene is where the heart of the vampire lies in my film *Shadow of the Vampire*, meaning that the cinema itself with its unholy trinity comprising the motion picture camera, the projector and the director are the true vampiric monsters. It was in post-production of *Shadow of the Vampire* that I saw it as a gesture of High Magic when I took original camera negative of Willem Dafoe as Schreck and using an optical printer I took the very fine flame of a blow torch to that original negative burning it, while I filmed those seven frames being burnt to ash. Ultimately these seven frames became the death scene in my film. The magic that I speak of is that you have the film director (me) burning the film's original negative and filming the burning of the original negative of his own film's movie star in order to create the death of this new Nosferatu – the cinema.

Q. In an article on your first film *Begotten* (1991) for Movie Scope magazine you write: 'I ask you to look at the motion picture camera/projector not as a machine or a tool, but as a cipher, a door, into the innermost workings of the universe itself.' Would you consider this approach to be also relevant in *Shadow of the Vampire*?

A. I would say that this is true of my entire approach to making films. There is some process in me that recognises the technology of film as an extension of my own spiritual sense of the deeper nature and deeper penetration into understanding what it means to be alive in this dream that is manufactured by our biological substance. With the motion picture we are able to extend our eyes to places that were previously invisible in all the centuries before its invention. Not only do optics allow us to see deeper than ever into space and even deeper into the microscopic formats of things but we have film emulsions that allows us to see X-rays, gamma rays, infrared light waves. We are able to slow down time, make it stop, make it freeze, we are able to speed up time, make days and weeks and years pass in seconds. The cinema is a cosmos created by man to the genius of technology. It is precursor and foundation to all the virtual worlds that we begun to enter into the twenty-first century.

I find myself at this moment extremely melancholic realising that when I made *Shadow of the Vampire* I was shooting with real film, real emulsion, nothing digital. I felt so much closer to the days of Murnau, of *Nosferatu*, and now I feel so much more distant, unchained from the analogue as the film as exists today is moving almost entirely into digital age.

Q. In the audio commentary of *Shadow of the Vampire* you mention a series of esoteric details and references scattered around the film. What is their function?

A. I have a small group of friends, all of us esotericists with whom I studied many texts in alchemy and the hermetic tradition. We also studied the Tarot and when the time came to making *Shadow of the Vampire* I wanted to infuse this film with esoteric subplots. One of them being the creation of a new *grimoire* filled with ciphers that would be my answer in my conversation with Albin Grau's use of symbols and ciphers as a means of using magic symbols in his *grimoire* in *Nosferatu*. Albin Grau was a deeply spiritual man, some of his closest friends were great esotericists of the time. A follower of the Ordo Templi Orientis (Order of the Temple of the East) he actually filmed Aleister Crowley in 1925. That film of Crowley has somehow disappeared. I felt it important when I created my *grimoire* for *Shadow of the Vampire* to create a living body of symbols that would communicate backward through time opening the door to a living conversation that would exist between my film and *Nosferatu*. Strangely the *grimoire* that was created for my film never made it into the movie. I did shoot scenes with Udo Kier as Albin Grau showing his preliminary drawings for his *grimoire*, and also showing him throw the Tarot to predict the destiny of the filming of *Nosferatu* but in the end the scene seemed too laborious and out of place, stalling the narrative during the final edit of *Shadow of the Vampire*. One of my closest friends, Leigh McCloskey, who himself is an artist and accomplished esotericist had at the time created for me a very special *grimoire* that emerged out of very many conversations he and I were having, conversations that focused around the esoteric implications of the film that I was setting out to make. Though this *grimoire* painted and created by Leigh never made it into my film, it eventually (years later) caught the attention of Keith Richards and made it into the collective psyche by being admired by The Rolling Stones who used its images in their live show.

In *Shadow of the Vampire* the inn which the cast and crew of *Nosferatu* stay in is called 'Han Budala' which would roughly translate in a Slavic language to 'The Inn of the Fool'. In my mind this is representative of the 'Fool' card in the Tarot which to me represents the foundation of all great creative inquiry. It was also the dominant card interpreting a future outcome for the making of *Shadow of the Vampire* when I threw the Tarot before casting and making the film. As an interesting coincidence preceding the casting and shooting of *Shadow of the Vampire* I was on the flight from Los Angeles to New York. The gentleman sitting next to me made inquiry about my reading of a *Shadow of the Vampire* screenplay. He was quite astonished to tell me of his fiancée who was the great great niece of Walter Spies, the great love of Murnau's life.

I conceived Schreck's cave with an alchemical depiction of the sun painted in the background. The sun in my mind, being the representative of the projector lamp of the cosmos and the cave itself being the archetypal source of all projection, the 'primal cinema'. Even the gift of blood given to Schreck by Murnau is contained in the old hand blown alchemical alembic used by early alchemists.

Q. Has your relationship with Murnau changed in the years that have passed after completing your film?

A. My relationship to Murnau's work has only deepened over the years, like the leitmotif that returns perennially reminding me of how timeless and beautiful Murnau's work is. I particularly enjoy watching *Sunrise* and *Tabu* for these films resonate with the timeless ache for love.

Q. Does the subject of vampirism still interest you or *Shadow of the Vampire* was the result of a very specific but circumscribed interest of yours?

A. What attracted me to *Shadow of the Vampire* was that the material lent itself to me in a way I can go beyond just making a genre film. Making a genre vampire movie held little interest to me, yet the bigger questions on the nature of vampirism and its relationship to art making and being an artist in general very much appealed to me. I can say that taking the material of *Shadow of the Vampire* away from the traditional vampire genre and making it my own is what excited me the most.

(Los Angeles, March 2015)

NOTES

1. Elsaesser, *Weimar Cinema*, p. 235.
2. Gunning, 'To Scan a Ghost', *Grey Room*, 2007, p. 97.
3. Rhodes, 'Drakula Halla', *Horror Studies*, pp. 25-47.
4. Weitz, *Weimar Germany*, p. 28.
5. Weitz, *Weimar Germany*, p. 207.
6. Roberts, *German Expressionist Cinema*, p. 3.
7. Dalle Vacche, *Cinema and Painting*, p. 167.
8. Thompson, *Eisenstein's Ivan the Terrible*, p. 173.
9. Grau, *Vampires*, Eureka DVD booklet, pp. 59-60.
10. Grau, *Vampires*, Eureka DVD booklet, p. 61.
11. Borst, *Graven Images*, p. 16-7.
12. Skal, *Hollywood Gothic*, p. 83.
13. Eisner, *Murnau*, p. 227.
14. Eisner, *Haunted Screen*, p. 101.
15. Eisner, *Haunted Screen*, p. 102.
16. Eisner, *Murnau*, pp. 13-4.
17. Shepard, *Nosferatu in Love*, p. 71.
18. Elsaesser, *Weimar Cinema*, p. 226.
19. Grau, *Buhne und Film*, 1921, no. 21.
20. http://www.filmhistoriker.de/films/nosferatu.htm Accessed on 19th September 2013.
21. http://www.filmhistoriker.de/films/nosferatu.htm Accessed on 19th September 2013.
22. http://www.filmhistoriker.de/films/nosferatu.htm Accessed on 19th September 2013.
23. Quoted in Skal, *Hollywood Gothic*, p. 83.
24. Skal, *Hollywood Gothic*, p. 89.
25. Skal, *Hollywood Gothic*, p. 97.
26. Tropp, *Images of Fear*, p. 134.
27. Stoker, *Dracula*, p. 334.
28. Brennan, 'Repression, Knowledge, and Saving Souls: the Role of the 'New Woman' in Stoker's *Dracula* and Murnau's *Nosferatu*', *Studies in the Humanities*, 1992, p. 2.
29. Stoker, *Dracula*, pp. 44-5.
30. Ashbury, *Nosferatu*, p. 22.
31. Billson, *Gothic*, p. 10.
32. Leatherdale, *Dracula*, p. 121.
33. Stoker, *Dracula*, p. 306.
34. Stoker, *Dracula*, p. 307.
35. Stoker, *Dracula*, p. 311.

36. Stoker, *Dracula*, p. 313.

37. Ashbury, *Nosferatu*, p. 17.

38. Carroll, *Philosophy of Horror*, p. 99.

39. Eisner, *Murnau*, p. 236.

40. Jackson, *Nosferatu*, p. 52.

41. '19a Hyena. 19b Horses, panicking'.

42. On a more light-hearted side note, this also starts a tradition of incongruously out of context animals inhabiting the vampire's castle that is reiterated in Tod Browning's adaptation of 1931 where a couple of armadillos and a tiny bee provided with a custom-made coffin roam the grounds of Dracula's dwelling.

43. Carroll, *Philosophy of Horror*, p. 100.

44. Keller, *The Bridge*, Eureka DVD booklet, p. 77.

45. Eisner, *Murnau*, p. 242.

46. Eisner, *Murnau*, p. 242.

47. http://www.mcsweeneys.net/articles/contest-winner-36-black-and-white-and-in-color Accessed 6th July 2013.

48. Jackson, *Nosferatu*, p. 55.

49. Stoker, *Dracula*, p. 35.

50. Eisner, *Murnau*, p. 243.

51. Eisner, *Murnau*, p. 243.

52. Eisner, *Murnau*, p. 244.

53. Jackson, *Nosferatu*, p. 62.

54. Eisner, *Murnau*, p. 245.

55. Eisner, *Murnau*, p. 246.

56. Eisner, *Murnau*, p. 247.

57. Carroll, *Philosophy of Horror*, p. 100.

58. Eisner, *Murnau*, p. 248.

59. Eisner, Murnau, p. 249

60. Jackson, *Nosferatu*, p. 71.

61. Gunning, 'To Scan a Ghost', *Grey Room*, 2007, p. 95.

62. Eisner, *Murnau*, p. 252.

63. Eisner, *Murnau*, p. 254.

64. Eisner, *Murnau*, p. 255.

65. Skal, *Hollywood Gothic*, p. 86.

66. Eisner, *Murnau*, p. 256.

67. Jackson, *Nosferatu*, p. 77.

68. Eisner, *Murnau*, p. 258.

69. Eisner, *Murnau*, p. 259.

70. Eisner, *Murnau*, p. 263.

71. Eisner, *Murnau*, p. 264.

72. Carroll, *Philosophy of Horror*, p. 101.

73. Eisner, *Murnau*, p. 264.

74. Eisner, *Murnau*, p. 265.

75. Stoker, *Dracula*, p. 339.

76. Eisner, *Murnau*, p. 269.

77. Jackson, *Nosferatu*, p. 93.

78. Eisner, *Haunted Screen*, p. 97.

79. Guillermo, 'Shadow and Substance', *Sight and Sound*, 1967, 36, p. 153.

80. Astruc, 'Fire and ice', *Cahiers du cinema in English*, 1966, 1, p. 71.

81. Gelder, *Reading the Vampire*, p. 95.

82. Rhode, *History of the Cinema*, p. 183.

83. Eisner, *Murnau*, pp. 85-6.

84. Murnau, 'Films of the Future', *McCall's Magazine*, 1928, p. 90.

85. Guillermo, 'Murnau', *Film Comment*, 1971, 7, p. 13.

86. Murnau, 'Films of the Future', *McCall's Magazine*, 1928, p. 90.

87. Luckhurst, *The Shining*, 2013, p. 10.

88. Dalle Vacche, *Cinema and Painting*, p. 165.

89. Eisenstein, 'The Montage of Attractions' (1923), in Taylor, *The Eisenstein Reader*, 2009, p. 30.

90. http://www.rogerebert.com/reviews/great-movie-nosferatu-1922 Accessed on 11th November 2014.

91. Robert Desnos, 'Nosferatu le Vampire', *Le Soir*, 1927, p.12.

92. Kracauer, *From Caligari to Hitler*, p. 107.

93. Kracauer, *From Caligari to Hitler*, p. 77.

94. Weitz, *Weimar Germany*, p. 321.

95. Eisner, *Murnau*, p. 18.

96. Kaes, *Shell Shock Cinema: Weimar Culture and the Wounds of War*, 2011.

97. Kaes, *Shell Shock Cinema*, p. 88.

98. Collier, *From Wagner to Murnau. The Transposition of Romanticism from Stage to Screen*, 1988.

99. Collier, *From Wagner to Murnau*, p. 110.

100. Stümke, 'The Persecution of Homosexuals in Nazi Germany' in Burleigh (ed.), *Confronting the Nazi Past*, 1996, pp. 154-5.

101. Paragraph 175 was entirely revoked from German law only in 1994.

102. Benshoff, *Monsters in the Closet*, p. 1.

103. Elsaesser, *Weimar Cinema*, p. 25.

104. Eisner, *Haunted Screen*, p. 100.

105. Eisner, *Haunted Screen*, p. 98.

106. Elsaesser, *Weimar Cinema*, p. 3.

107. Stoker, *Dracula*, p. 31.

108. Prawer, *Nosferatu*, p. 57 and Jackson, *Nosferatu*, p. 111.

109. Prawer, *Nosferatu*, p. 58.

110. Kyrou quoted in Elsaesser, 'No End to *Nosferatu*', p. 19.

111. Wehner, *Who Wrote That*, p. 34.

112. Vertov, *The Council of the Three*, p. 17.

113. Weinstock, *Vampire Film*, p. 87.

114. Tennyson, *Tithonus*, vv. 18-23.

115. Elsaesser, *No End to Nosferatu*, p. 23.

BIBLIOGRAPHY

Abbott, S (2007) *Celluloid Vampires: Life After Death in the Modern World.* Austin: University of Texas Press

Ashbury, R (2001) *Nosferatu.* London: Longman/York Press

Bell, J (ed.) (2013) *Gothic: the Dark Heart of Film.* London: BFI

Benshoff, H (1997) *Monsters in the Closet: Homosexuality and the Horror Film.* Manchester and New York: Manchester University Press

Berriatúa, L (1991) *Los Proverbios Chinos de F.W. Murnau.* Madrid: Filmoteca Española

Bordwell, D and Thompson, K (2010) *Film History: an Introduction.* New York: McGraw-Hill

Borst, R (1992) *Graven Images: the Best of Horror, Fantasy, and Science-Fiction Film Art from the Collection of Ronald V. Borst.* New York: Grove Press

Botting, F (1996) *Gothic.* London and New York: Routledge

Bouvier, M and Letraut, JL (1981) *Nosferatu.* Paris: Gallimard

Brakhage, S (1977) *Film Biographies.* Berkeley: Turtle Island

Breton, A (1955) *Les vases communicants.* Paris: Gallimard

--------- (1965) *Le surréalisme et la peinture.* Paris: Gallimard

Burnham Bloom, A (2010) *The Literary Monster on Film.* Jefferson: MacFarland

Callens, J (2006) '*Shadow of the Vampire*: Double Take on *Nosferatu*' in Chapple, F and Kattenbelt, C (eds.) *Intermediality in Theatre and Performance.* Amsterdam - New York: Rodopi

Carroll, N (1990) *The Philosophy of Horror.* London and New York: Routledge

Catania, S (2004) 'Absent Presences in Liminal Places: Murnau's *Nosferatu* and the Otherworld of Stoker's *Dracula*', *Literature/Film Quarterly.* Vol. 32 no. 3

Coats, P (1991) *The Gorgon's Gaze: German Cinema, Expressionism and the Image of Horror*. Cambridge: Cambridge University Press

Collier, J (1988) *From Wagner to Murnau: the Transposition of Romanticism from Stage to Screen*. Ann Arbor: UMI

Dalle Vacche, A (1996) *Cinema and Painting: How Art is Used in Film*. Austin: University of Texas Press

Eisner, L (1973) *Murnau*. London: Secker & Warburg

--------- (1973) *The Haunted Screen: Expressionism in the German Cinema and the Influence of Max Reinhardt*. Berkeley: University of California Press

Elsaesser, T (2000) *Weimar Cinema and After. Germany's Historical Imaginary*. London and New York: Routledge

--------- (2007) 'No End to *Nosferatu*' published in the booklet for the Eureka DVD of *Nosferatu* (2007)

Exertier, S (1980) 'La lettre oubliée de *Nosferatu*', *Positif*. No. 228

Franklin, J.C (1980) 'Metamorphosis of a Metaphor: the Shadow in Early German Cinema', *The German Quarterly*. Vol. 53 no. 2

Frayling, C (1991) *Vampyres: Lord Byron to Count Dracula*. London: Faber and Faber

Gelder, K (1994) *Reading the Vampire*. London and New York: Routledge

--------- (2012) *New Vampire Cinema*. London: Palgrave Macmillan

Grau, A (1921) 'Vampires', *Buhne und Film*. No. 21; trans. Craig Keller and published in the booklet for the Eureka DVD of *Nosferatu* (2007)

Gunning, T (2007) 'To Scan a Ghost: the Ontology of Mediated Vision', *Grey Room*. No. 26

Hennelly, M (undated) 'Betwixt Sunset and Sunrise: Liminality in *Dracula*'. www.blooferland.com/drc/images/07Hennell.rtf (accessed September 8th 2014)

Hensley, W. E (2002) 'The Contribution of F.W. Murnau's *Nosferatu* to the Evolution of Dracula', *Literature/Film Quarterly*. Vol. 30 no. 1

Jackson, K (2013) *Nosferatu. Eine Symphonie des Grauens*. London: Palgrave Macmillan

Jameaux, C (1965) *Murnau*. Paris: Éditions Universitaires

Käser, R and Pohland, V (eds.) (1990) *Disease and Medicine in Modern German Cultures*. Ithaca N.Y.: Cornell University Press

Keller, C (2007) 'The Bridge' published in the booklet for the Eureka DVD of *Nosferatu* (2007)

Kracauer, S (1947) *From Caligari to Hitler: A Psychological History of German Film*. Princeton: Princeton University Press

Merhige, E. E (undated) 'The Dark Soul of Cinema', *Movie Scope Magazine*

Murch, W (2006) 'Black and White and in Color', McSweeneys

Murnau, F.W (1928) 'Films of the Future', *McCall's Magazine*. September Issue

Patalas, E (2002) 'On the Way to *Nosferatu*' published in the booklet for the Eureka DVD of *Nosferatu* (2007)

Perez Guillermo, G (1967) 'Shadow and Substance: Murnau's *Nosferatu*', *Sight and Sound*. Vol. 36 no. 3

--------- (1971) 'F.W. Murnau: an Introduction', *Film Comment*. Vol. 7 no. 2

--------- (1998) 'The Deadly Space Between' published in the booklet for the Eureka DVD of *Nosferatu* (2007)

Prawer, S.S (2013) *Nosferatu: Phantom der Nacht*. London: Palgrave Macmillan

Rhodes, G. D (2010) '*Drakula halla* (1921): The Cinema's First Dracula', *Horror Studies*. Vol. 1 no. 1

Ricks, C (ed.) (2007) *Selected Poems: Tennyson*. London: Penguin

Roberts, I (2008) *German Expressionist Cinema: the World of Light and Shadow*. New York: Wallflower Press

Shepard, J (1998) *Nosferatu in Love*. London: Faber

Skal, D (1990) *Hollywood Gothic: The Tangled Web of Dracula from Stage to Screen*. New York: Norton

Stoker, B (1993) *Dracula*. London: Penguin

Tropp, M (1999) *Images of Fear: How Horror Stories Helped Shape Modern Culture, 1818-1918*. Jefferson, NC: McFarland

Stümke, H. G (1996) 'The Persecution of Homosexuals in Nazi Germany' in Burleigh, M (ed.) *Confronting the Nazi Past*. London: Collins and Brown

Unrau, R (1996) 'Eine Symphonie des Grauens or The Terror of Music: Murnau's *Nosferatu*', *Literature/Film Quarterly*. Vol. 24 no. 3

Vertov, D (1923) 'The Council of the Three' in Michelson, A (ed.) (1984) *Kino-Eye: the Writings of Dziga Vertov* London and Sydney: Pluto Press

Wehner, C. C (2003) *Who Wrote That Movie? Screenwriting in Review 2000-2002*. Bloomington: Universie

Weinstock, J (2012) *The Vampire Film: Undead Cinema*. London: Wallflower

Weitz, E (2013) *Weimar Germany: Promise and Tragedy*. Princeton: Princeton University Press

Whitney, A (2010) 'Etched with the Emulsion: Weimar Dance and Body Culture in German Expressionist Cinema', *Seminar: A Journal of Germanic Studies*. Vol. 46 no. 3

Printed and bound by CPI Group (UK) Ltd, Croydon, CR0 4YY

27/03/2025

14649115-0001